Papers on Historical

Algonquian
and
Iroquois Topics

By
David A. Ezzo
Michael H. Moskowitz

17th Century Algonquian Man. Painting by Shinnecock artist David Bunn Martine. Used by permission of the artist.

First published by Dog Ear Publishing
4010 W. 86th Street, Ste H
Indianapolis, IN 46268
www.dogearpublishing.net

ISBN: 978-159858-343-4

This book is printed on acid-free paper.

Printed in the United States of America

Contents

ACKNOWLEDGEMENTS

It is a difficult task to thank all the people who have supported and encouraged my studies. First, I would like to thank my long time friend and mentor Mr. Ronald P. Koch. It was Ron who first introduced me to the subject of Native Americans when I took the BSA Indian Lore merit badge under him. I also must thank Ron for editing several of the chapters in this book.

I also must thank several of my teachers at SUNY Fredonia. First, I would like to thank Dr. William T. Hagan. Dr. Hagan served as the teacher for my first course on North American Indian History as well as a course on Western History. I must also thank my two Anthropology teachers at SUNY Fredonia, Dr. Alvin H. Morrison and Dr. Alan G. LaFlamme.

Both Dr. Morrison and Dr. LaFlamme were teachers for many Anthropology courses that I took as an Anthropology major at SUNY Fredonia. It was Dr. Morrison who asked me to co-author a paper with him for the 16th Algonquian Conference. This paper began my association with the annual Algonquian Conference. If it wasn't for Dr. Morrison I might not have ever attended and presented papers at the Algonquian Conferences.

I also must acknowledge the Department of Anthropology at the University of Oklahoma for the support that I received as a graduate student for two years during the time I was working on my MA degree. I would like to thank my thesis committee: Dr. Joseph Whitecotton, Dr. Betty Harris, Dr. Stephen Thompson arid Dr. John Moore for all their help and guidance during my two years at the University of Oklahoma.

I would also like to note the support that I received from a few of my fellow students, especially Danielle Moretti-Langholtz and Greg Campbell.

1 would like to note that all of the chapters in this book began as papers that were presented at annual Algonquian Conferences. I must also note the support and help from my co-author, Michael Moskowitz. It has been a real joy and pleasure to work with my best friend on several of these chapters in our book

I would also like to thank my parents, Albert and Ann Ezzo for all of their support and guidance. Without their help I would never have come this far. I would like to thank the support of my wife, Michelle Ezzo. Without her support this book would not have been possible.

Last I would like to thank Nicole Guile for typing our book into Microsoft word format thus preparing our book for publication.

David A. Ezzo
Kenmore, New York
March 2007

Putting a written work together on a subject that one deeply cares about is usually the end result of many years of experience with the topic. But in order to sustain the effort you usually have many people who have educated you, supported you and directed you to this point.

For me it was no different, and in that vein I would like to thank first my immediate family, my late parents, Leonard and Sheila Moskowitz, for turning me on to a love of history, politics, geography and law; my sister and brother-in-law, Renee and Daniel Sussman for continued support; and of course to my wife, Beth Zimelman, who completes me with her love and continued inspiration and encouragement.

I have to thank my co-author and friend, David Ezzo for getting me involved in a very serious way with this subject. While, like David, I have been active in Scouting for many years and enjoyed the Native American related information that it's a part of the program, it was David that moved me along from just instructing young people on the subject to writing about it with him for the Algonquian Conferences.

As a law student at American University in Washington, D.C. I was lucky enough to learn from Prof. Nell Newton the uniqueness and complexity of the laws that cover American Indian nations and individuals. It was through her class and guidance that I developed the knowledge and connections to work in this field.

Finally, I would have to thank the numerous Native Americans I have had the pleasure of working with over the years both in Washington, D.C. and here on Long Island in New York State.

Michael H. Moskowitz
Wantagh, NY
March, 2007

Chapter 1:

Female Status in the Northeast

Ethnohistorical evidence indicates that females had a variety of important functions in Native northeastern societies, and that they were important social actors who had power in the public sphere of these societies. I propose a model for female status which I believe applies to all of these northeastern societies. There are three basic parts to my model of female status. The first part of the model, and a primary factor in determining female status in all of these societies, is the life cycle. In each of these societies older females who were past middle age were the only females mentioned in the ethnohistorical literature who had individual power in the public sphere. The second part of the model, and in my opinion, the second primary factor that determines female status (or public power) is resource control. Each of the older, individual females that are recorded in the ethnohistorical literature had control over resources — trade goods, agricultural products and goods, or special knowledge of herbs and medicines. Thus I am using the term "resources" in a broad sense. The last part of the model are the structural factors that work to reinforce and maintain female status in the society. The structural factors include: matrilineal descent, matrilocal residence, male absence, rules of succession, domestic living arrangements and the presence of a female deity. Thus this model relates the individual female, resource control and the infrastructure of a society together to understand how, why and under what particular circumstances individual females were able to wield public power.

The Wabanaki

The ethnohistorical record on the Wabanaki discusses individual females who were known as "grand-dames" or *Nokomums*. These females were past middle age and had a variety of privileges that younger females did not have. They also had more mobility, freedom from restraint and were able to serve in a variety of important positions in Wabanakia, including functioning as political leaders or speakers in council and serving as shamans (Chamberlain 1902:85-86; Morrison 1983:126-127). The ethno-historical record illustrates that a number of Wabanaki females inherited formal leadership positions. Angel Queen, a female sagamore-shaman was an older woman who is reported to have traveled to Wabanaki villages at least twice each year. She was a powerful shaman who distributed food as she traveled among the villages. This individual Wabanaki female was an older woman who had control over both food resources and was reported to have strong magical power and thus had power as a shaman as well (Morrison 1983:129).

There are also several other individual females who are recorded in the ethnohistorical literature who clearly had individual public power. The Queene of Quacke was a female leader who inherited her leadership position from her father (Levett 1893:104-105). Another female who inherited a leadership position was Jacataqua of Swan Island who inherited the position of sagamore from her mother. Both of these females illustrate that one of the structural features present in Wabanakia that worked to reinforce and maintain female status were rules of succession that allowed individual females to inherit formal leadership positions (Morrison 1983:130; Griffiths 1976).

The elder Penobscot shaman Molly Molasses was respected and feared as a very powerful shaman. Both her age and her knowledge of herbs and medicines enabled her to obtain a position of public power and influence (Eckstorm 1980:21). Another older female religious leader who had great power in Micmac society was recorded by Christian missionary Le Clercq. This female religious leader was recorded in the ethnohistorical literature as having the power to cure the sick and protect people from enemies. Thus by having earned the reputation of being a powerful shaman, this woman was able to achieve a position of power in the public sphere of Wabanaki society (Le Clercq 1910:229-230; Axtell 1981:193-194).

Thus even though agriculture was only practiced in the southern section of Wabanakia, females were able to obtain positions of power in the society by becoming shamans and inheriting leadership positions. The females that were recorded in the ethnohistorical literature were older, a fact which enabled them to function as shamans, council speakers and political leaders because they were also able to control resources in their society. The structural organization of Wabankia aided these females by having rules of succession for political office that allowed females to inherit positions of leadership. These females were aided by this rule, but none of them would have achieved a position of power in the public sphere of the society without also being an elder who had control over resources.

FEMALE STATUS IN THE NORTHEAST

The Delaware

Female Delaware are recorded in the ethnohistorical literature as serving in a number of important roles in Delaware society. Older females and a group of young men were able to force the Esopus war captains to seek peace with the Dutch in 1664 (Grumet 1980:52). Older females were also important as shamans and traders in Delaware society.

Here again individual females were able to attain positions of power in Delaware society only because they were older and had control over important resources like agricultural or trade goods or shamanic curing powers. Clearly, elder female shamans who had the power to communicate with the dead, locate lost persons and fortell future events had individual power in the religious sphere of Delaware society. The economic importance of coastal Algonquian females as recorded by Mourt (1841), Heckewelder (1817), Juet (1909) and a trader at Albany also can not be overlooked.

Female status in Delaware society was reinforced and maintained by a number of important structural factors including agriculture, matrilineal descent, matrilocal residence and the ritual cycle. Corn was the major staple of the Delaware diet and since females worked the garden and controlled the distribution of the agricultural products, this worked to reinforce female status in the society. Female status was also supported and reinforced by the 12 matrilineal lineages that were present in Delaware society. These lineages regulated marriage, ceremonial obligations, feasts and the inheritance of special ritual property (Goddard 1978:225).

Individual females were very important as shamans in Delaware society and the Delaware ritual cycle also worked to maintain and reinforce female status. The two important types of ceremonies were family feasts and vision rituals. A major ceremony was held at both corn planting and harvesting time and females played an important role in the ceremony (Goddard 1978:231-232). The matrilineal lineages conducted annual ceremonies which also gave support to female status and reinforced the position of high status for females in Delaware society.

The Shawnee

Females in Shawnee society served in a variety of functions and influenced war chiefs, supervised village affairs, directed the planting, cooking and accompanment of the feasts. In all parts of Shawnee society where females served as important social actors in the public sphere the key elements of my model are all present.

Agriculture was important in Shawnee society and it clearly worked to reinforce and maintain female status. The two distinct women's committees that directed the Brad Dance feasts were the *Naynahowaychki* and the *Mayyawwathechki*. The life cycle (or age) was the key factor in the selection of females for the *Mayyawwathechki* committee. The ritual cycle itself reinforced female status in Sliawnee society since the Bread dance was a ceremony conducted for crop fertility. The females were the ones who called for the ceremony and the women also distributed the meat the feast itself (Galloway 1934:190).

Older women also decided the fate of Shawnee war captives and a individual elder female could serve as a ritual war leader if she had a vision that gave her specific instructions (Trowbridge 1939:26). Thus here again an individual elder female could obtain a position of power in the public sphere of society if she also had received a vision which therefore gave her supernatural power. Female status in Shawnee society was also reinforced by their religious system which featured an important deity called "our Grandmother" (Voegelin and Voegelin 1944; Alford 1979).

The Montagnais

Montagnais females were considered to have equal status to males in the society and personal autonomy for both sexes was reinforced by a number of structural factors present in the social structure of Montagnais society.

In Montagnais bands, each member of the group was dependent upon each other and "Obedience was owed not to any individual, but to the practical and moral order of the group" (Leacock 1981:191-193). In Montagnais society leadership in any particular situation was allowed to fall upon the shoulders of the individual who was most knowledgeable. The principal of personal autonomy for both sexes was present in Montagnais society and it was supported by a number of structural features of Montagnais social organization. There was no rigid sexual division of labour and decisions were made by the household group. Polygamy was allowed for both sexes and divorce was easy for either marriage partner. Both men and women were involved in running the household and males were also very involved with the raising of the children. The reciprocal exchange of goods and services in Montagnais society also worked to reinforce and maintain sexual equality in the society. Both women and men held their own feasts and the women as well as the males were involved in the torture of war captives. Thus the entire social structure of Montagnais society reinforced and maintained sexual equality and personal autonomy.

In Montagnais society, older females could obtain positions of influence in the society by controlling resources. Older females in the society functioned as both shamans and village supervisors. Older females who had a good knowledge of herbs and medicines functioned as healers and thus obtained a position of personal influence in the society. Female village supervisors decided the course of the bands and thus functioned as household leaders. Although there was a tendency for matrilocal residence in Montagnais society, postnuptial residence was quite flexible. The flexibility of Montagnais society is also illustrated by the fact that no formal kinship groups or clans were present.

The personal autonomy and sexual equality that was present in Montagnais society is illustrated by the ethnohistorical evidence. Information found in the *Jesuit Relations* supports the structural features of Montagnais society that I have discussed. Women in the accounts are discussed as co-equals of males and are said to have great influence over their husbands. The accounts also describe the very flexible division of labour in Montagnais society, female control over their own products, the right to divorce and polygamy for both sexes. This independence and personal autonomy of Montagnais females was deplored by the European missionaries and is discussed at some length in the literature (Thwaites 1906:2:77; Leacock 1980:27; Burgess 1944:4-7).

Thus females in Montagnais society were equals to males and the sexual equality present in the society was reinforced and maintained by the key factors of the social structure that I have mentioned and by an economy that was based on the reciprocal exchange of goods and services between the sexes. Individual Montagnais females who were older could become powerful shamans in the society and thus wield individual influence in the society. These females were able to become shamans because of their age and special supernatural power. Older females in Montagnais society also served as village supervisors who organized the camp and distributed the supplies (Thwaites 1906:6:61, 14:183; Rogers and Leacock 1981:182).

Thus, female status in Montagnais society operated on two different levels. At the individual level a particular female could become a shaman or village supervisor. Female status in the society as a whole was maintained by the flexible social organization and a variety of structural factors that allowed Montagnais females to be considered co-equals with males. All of this changed once contact with the Europeans and in particular the missionaries began, and female status at both the individual and collective level began to decline.

Before great changes began to be imposed on Montagnais society due to European contact, females did indeed function in important positions as, individually and collectively, females were considered to be co-equals with males. On the individual level the only females in Montagnais society who achieved positions of power in the society were older females who also controlled resources. On a societal level, females were considered to be equal to males and the structural features of Montagnais social organization as well as the reciprocal exchange of goods and services present in the Montagnais band economy both helped to maintain and reinforce collective female status in Montagnais society. Thus the model I have proposed focuses on both individual and collective female status within Montagnais society. Both of these aspects of female status must be understood in order to achieve a more accurate historical picture of how females functioned within Montagnais society.

The Iroquois

Females had higher status in Iroquoian society than in any of the other groups that I have discussed. In order to understand why females had such high status in Iroquois society, the structural factors which were present in Iroquois society that served to maintain and reinforce female status must be understood.

In Iroquois society, as in all of the other groups that I have discussed, female status operated on two levels, the individual and the collective. In Iroquois society, all the individual females who achieved a position of power in the public sphere of the society were elders who had control over resources. Individual females functioned as shamans, ritual warfare leaders and traders in Iroquoian society. Thus in Iroquoian society older females who had control over resources were able to wield personal power in the public sphere of the society (Thwaites 1896:44:37). The key structural factors that were present in Iroquois society included matrilineal descent, matrilocal residence, male absence, the domestic living arrangements and female power to elect and terminate male political leaders. The Iroquoian economy, which was based on agricultural production that was done by the females also helped to maintain and reinforce collective female status because the females controlled the production and distribution of the agricultural goods (Brown 1970; Kent and Deardorff 1960:465; Rothenberg 1980:80).

From the household and the domestic living arrangements of the long-house to the matrilineal clan system, collective female status was maintained and reinforced by a variety of structural factors present in Iroquois society. These structural features functioned to create strong groups of politically powerful females (the matrons) while they served to isolate the males in the society (Brown 1970; Randle 1951; Fenton 1986:36-38).

The Iroquois leaders were males but they were elected and could be put out of office by the female matrons who not only controlled the agricultural goods but they also held all the titles, rights and property. When a female died property was inherited by her children. The females were also in charge of the longhouse and distributed the food to the Iroquois families (Morgan 1965:65; Rothenberg 1980:69)

Another structural feature that was present in Iroquois society that helped to maintain and increase female status was male absence. The Iroquois females actually gained in status due to contact with the Europeans during the fur trade period because males were away from the village on either hunting or warfare expeditions. Thus the Iroquois are the only society that I have discussed in which the females actually gained in status for a period of time after contact with the Europeans (Rothenberg 1981:67; Leacock 1983; Trigger 1978).

Since Iroquois females controlled the land, agricultural tools and the means of production, they were able to become more involved in political decision making (collectively). They also had great influence over Iroquois war parties since they controlled the provisions that supplied these expeditions. The surplus agricultural products were exchanged intertribally and this allowed females to become more involved in decision making on the collective level (Parker 1912:234-236; Rothenberg 1981:69).

Iroquois matrons had a variety of powers including influencing war parties, speaking in council, conferring titles and electing officials, removing officials, serving as ambassadors and determining issues of war and peace in times of crisis (Fenton 1986:36-38).

Thus the model that I have used to examine female status operates on both the individual and collective level in Iroquoian society. Although individual females were able to achieve positions of power in all of the societies that I have discussed by being older females who controlled resources; none of the females in the other societies I have mentioned held such collective power in their society as did females in Iroquois society. Iroquois society had a more complex web of structural factors that worked to provide females with a higher collective status than was found any where else in native North America.

Collective Female Status: The Montagnais

Of the five northeastern groups that I have discussed in this paper, females had the lowest collective status in Montagnais society. By using the term "collective female status" I am referring to situations where groups of females were important and wielded power.

Montagnais society was based on personal autonomy for both sexes and leadership was flexible and fell to a particular individual that was best suited to lead in a specific situation. Although females did obtain positions of personal power by functioning as shamans and village supervisors, Montagnais society did not have the structural features like matrilineal descent, matrilocal residence, clans, etc. that allow for the formation of powerful groups of females.

The ethnohistorical record only illustrates that individual females were important as shamans and village supervisors. The infrastructure of Montagnais society that was based on flexible postnuptial residence and division of labour, and personal autonomy for both sexes was not one that would allow for the formation of group alliances. Thus the ethnohistorical record that stressed the importance of individual Montagnais females as opposed to groups of females must be viewed within the context of the structural factors that were present in Montagnais society.

The Wabanaki

Females in Wabanaki society had only slightly more collective status and power than females in Montagnais society. The only area in Wabanaki society in which females played an important collective role was in the ritual torture of war captives. This was done by females in Wabanaki society and they participated as a group in the Scalp Dance which honored specific warriors who had taken scalps or captives. Thus collective female importance in the torture or war captives was reinforced by the ritual cycle in Wabanaki society (Morrison 1982:13).

Wabanaki society did not have any of the structural features which contribute to the formation of powerful collective groups of females. Thus it is not surprising that the vast majority of the ethnohistorical record focused on important individual Wabanaki females and not on the power that groups of females in Wabanaki society had.

The Shawnee

Females functioned as important collective groups in several areas in Shawnee society. Agriculture was practiced by the Shawnee and it was a very important part of Shawnee subsistence. One of the areas in which Shawnee females were important as a collective group was in the Bread Dance feast which was a ceremony conducted for crop fertility. The females called the ceremony, distributed the meat at the feast and two women's committees directed the feast (Callender 1978; Trowbridge 1939:12, 13).

Shawnee females also decided the fate of Shawnee war captives. Four older females were the heads of the female society that decided the fate of Shawnee war captives. (Trowbridge 1939:13, 26). Although collective female status was supported to a degree by the importance of agriculture in the Shawnee subsistence economy and the ritual cycle, Shawnee society did not have the key structural factors that allow for the formation of female alliance groups that can wield a great deal of collective power.

The Delaware

Matrilocal had a high degree of collective status in Delaware society because the structural factors that allow for the formation of collective groups of allied females were present. The most important features in Delaware society that supported collective female status were matrilineal descent, matrilocal residence and the importance of agriculture.

The ethnohistorical record describes a variety of areas in which females were important as collective groups. A group of females helped to force the Esopus war captains to seek peace with the Dutch. This can be understood since females controlled the production and distribution of the agricultural goods that supplied the war parties (Grumet 1980:52).

The ethnohistorical record also shows that females were important as traders in a number of coastal Algonquian groups. Females were also able to regulate marriages, ceremonial obligations, feasts and the inheritance of special ritual property in Delaware society because of the presence of the matrilineal lineages.

The Iroquois

Females had a higher level of collective status in Iroquoian society than in any of the other northeastern groups that I have discussed. Iroquois society had a number of structural features that maintained collective female status including matrilineal descent, matrilocal residence, matrilineal clans, agriculture, male absence and the power of the matrons to elect and terminate male political leaders (Goldenweiser 1912:468). All of these structural features allowed females to have tremendous collective power in Iroquois society including: the control over Iroquois war parties, trade goods, agricultural goods, titles, rights, property and the household (Brown 1970; Morgan 1965:65-66).

Conclusion

In conclusion, the ethnohistorical evidence discussed in this paper clearly illustrates that females functioned in a wide variety of roles as social actors in both the domestic sphere and the public sphere of these native societies. Females in these Northeastern groups served as political leaders, shamans, ritual warfare leaders, village supervisors, council speakers and traders. I think that through the use of ethnohistory and by using a variety of primary source materials a much more accurate picture of how females functioned historically in native North American can be obtained. Before an accurate picture of how these native societies functioned historically can be constructed, however, the roles of females in these societies must be discovered. The traditional notion that females were important only in the domestic sphere of a particular society is falsified by the evidence from the ethnohistorical literature. Thus by documenting the variety of roles that females had in native North America, the first step in achieving a more accurate picture of how these Native societies functioned historically is achieved.

I have proposed a model of female status that focuses on both individual and collective female status. The two key components of this model of female status are the life cycle (age) and resource control. In all of these Northeastern groups, individual females who achieved positions of power in the public sphere of society were elders who also controlled important resources (agricultural, trade, or supernatural power). Thus this is a constant found among all of these Northeastern groups that I have discussed.

The other component of my model of female status is the structural factors that were present in these particular societies that functioned to maintain and reinforce collective female status. The collective level of female status was the highest in Iroquoian society because of the number of structural factors that worked together to maintain female status. Thus the strength of collective female status varied between these Northeastern groups depending upon the particular structural features that were present in each of these societies.

I also believe that that "male supremacist complex" that has been proposed by Divale and Harris (1977) has been exaggerated. Although the Micmac, Maliseet-Passamaquoddy and Montagnais all had a subsistence pattern that was supported mostly by hunting, and no agriculture was practiced in these groups, individual females still achieved positions of power in the public sphere of these societies. Thus even among nonagricultural native groups, individual females were important in the public sphere of society and did not function historically only in the domestic sphere of these societies.

I think that gaining a better understanding of the variety of roles that females had in native North America is only a first step in the more important process of constructing a more accurate historical picture of how both sexes functioned within these native groups. By understanding the roles of both sexes within these societies a more accurate historical picture can be composed.

Research of female status is a good laboratory that can allow the anthropologist to study the process of historical change in native societies. By doing comparative research that focuses on how female status changed as a result of contact with the world system, a better understanding of how the social structure of native societies was changed by the world system can be achieved.

It is also true as Katerine Weist (1982:46) has pointed out that the treatment of Indian women was a major factor for the designation of the term "savage". By using ethnohistorical methods to study primary source accounts, a more accurate picture of the role of females in native society can be achieved. Alfred Miller once stated that "nothing so strikingly distinguishes civilized from savage life as the treatment of women. It is in every particular in favor of the former." (1968:70). This viewpoint is not upheld by the ethnohistorical evidence that I have presented in this paper that shows that female status declined as a result of contact with civilization.

In short, I believe that there is still much more work that needs to be done in this area. The cross-cultural study of female status is merely the first step that is required in order to achieve a more accurate historical picture of how these Northeastern societies functioned. Before a more accurate historical picture of these native societies can be achieved the roles of females in these groups must be described. As Valerie Mathers stated "the historical surface has been barely scratched on the subject of Indian women." (1975:137). This is also true for much of native North America. I hope that in at least a small way, the material that I have presented on female status in these particular groups from the Northeast has helped to illustrate how females functioned in these groups.

REFERENCES

Alford, Thomas W.
  1936 *Civilization as Told to Florence Drake.* Norman: University of Oklahoma. Press.

Axtell, James
  1981 *The Indian Peoples of Eastern America: A Documentary History of the Sexes.* Oxford: Oxford University Press.

Brown, Judith K.
  1970 Economic Organization and the Position of Women Among the Iro-quois. *Ethnohistory* 17:151-167.

Burgesse, J. Allan
  1944 The Women and the Child Among the Lac-St. Jean Montagnais. *Primitive Man* 17:102-119.

Callender, Charles
  1978 Shawnee. Pp. 622-635 in *Handbook of North American Indians.* Vol. 15: Northeast. Bruce G. Trigger, ed. Washington: Smithsonian Institution.

Chamberlain, Montague
  1902   The Primitive Life of the Wapanaki Women. *Acadiensis* 2:75-86.

Divale, William T., and Marvin Harris
  1976 Population, Warfare and the Male Supremacist Complex. *American Anthropologist* 78:521-538.

Eckstorm, Fannie Hardy
  1980 *Old John Neptune and Other Maine Indian Shamans,* Orono, Maine: University of Maine Press. [Originally published 1945].

Fenton, William
  1986 Leadership in the Northeastern Woodlands of North America. *American Indian Quarterly,* Winter,
  pp. 21-44.

Galloway, William A.
  1934 *Old ChiUicothe: Shawnee and Pioneer History: Conflicts and Romances in the Northwest Territory.* Xenia, Ohio: Buckeye Press.

Goddard, Ives
　　1978　　Delaware.　Pp. 213-239 in *Handbook of North American Indians,* Vol. 15: Northeast. Bruce G. Trigger, ed. Washington: Smithsonian Institution.

Goldenweiser, Alexander
　　1912　　On Iroquois Work, 1912. Pp. 464-475 in *Summary Report of the Geological Survey of Canada, Anthropology Division, Sessional Paper* 26. Ottawa.

Griffiths, Linda
　　1976 Jactaqua. *Bates College Bulletin (Alumnus Issue)* 73:8

Grumet, Robert Steven
　　1980 Sunskquas, Shamans and Tradeswomen: Middle Atlantic Coastal Algonkian Women during the 17th and 18th Centuries. Pp. 43-62 in *Women and Colonization: Anthropological Perspectives.* Mona Etienne and Eleanor Leacock, eds. New York: Praeger.

Heckewelder, John
　　1817 *History, Manners, and Customs of the Indian Nations.* Philadelphia: Historical Society of Pennsylvania.

Juet, Robert
　　1909 From "The Third Voyage of Master Henry Hudson," 1610. Pp. 11-28 in *Narratives of New Netherland. 1609-1664.* J. Franklin Jameson, ed. New York: Charles Scribner and Sons.

Kent, Donald H., and Merle H. Deardorff
　　1960 John Adlum on the Allegheny: Memoirs for the Year 1794. *Pennsylvania Magazine of History and Biography* 84:265-324, 435-480.

Leacock, Eleanor
　　1980 Montagnais Women and the Jesuit Program for Colonization. Pp. 25-42 in *Women and Colonization: Anthropological Perspectives.* Mona Etienne and Eleanor Leacock, eds. New York: Praeger.

　　1981 Seventeenth Century Montagnais Social Relations and Values. Pp. 190-195 in *Handbook of North American Indians,* Vol. 6: Subarctic. June Helm, ed. Washington: Smithsonian Institution.

Le Clerq, Chrestien
　　1910 *New Relations of Gaspesia with the Customs & Religion of the Gaspe-sian Indians.* Edited and translated by William F. Ganong, Toronto: The Champlain Society. [Originally published 1691].

Levett, Christopher
1983 A Voyage into New England Begun in 1623 and Ended in 1624. Pp. 79-139 in *Christopher Levett of York. The Pioneer Colonist in Casco Bay.* James P. Baxter, ed. Portland, Maine: The Gorges Society. [Originally published 1628].

Mathers, Valerie S.
1975 A New Look at the Role of Women in Indian Society. *American Indian Quarterly* 2:131-139

Miller, Alfred J.
1968 *The West of Alfred Jacob Miller from the Notes and Water Colors in the Walters Art Gallery with an Account of the Artist by Marvin C. Ross.* Norman: University of Oklahoma Press.

Morgan, Lewis H.
1851 *League of the Ho-De-No-Sau-Nee, or Iroquois.* New York: Dodd, Mead and Company.
1965 *Houses and House — Life of the American Aborigines.* Chicago: University of Chicago Press.
1974 *Ancient Society.* Gloucester, Mass.: Peter Smith.

Morrison, Alvin H.
1982 Dawnland Dog-Feast: Wabanaki Warfare and Slavery, ca. 1600-ca. 1760. A Paper presented at the Canadian Ethnology Society, Vancouver, British Columbia.

Wabanaki Women Extraordinaire: A Sampler from Fact and Fancy.
1983 Pp. 125-136 in *Papers of the Fourteenth Algonquian Conference.* William Cowan, ed. Ottawa: Carleton University.

Mourt, George
1841 "Mourt's Relation". In *Chronicles of the Pilgrim Fathers of the Colony of Plymouth from 1602 to 1625.* Alexander Young, ed. Boston: Little and Brown. [Originally published 1622].

Parker, Arthur C.
1912 Iroquois Uses of Maize and Other Food Plants. *New York State Museum Bulletin* 144- Albany: University of the State of New York.

Randle, Martha C.
1951 Iroquois Women Then and Now. Pp. 167-180 in *Bulletin of the Bureau of American Ethnology* 149. Washington.

Rogers, Edward S., and Eleanor Leacock
   1981 Montagnais-Naskapi. Pp. 169-189 in *Handbook of North American Indians,* Vol. 6: Subarctic. June Helm, ed. Washington: Smithsonian Institution.

Rothenberg, Diana B.
   1980 The Mothers of the Nation. Pp. 63-87 in *Women and Colonization: Anthropological Perspectives.* Mona Etienne and Eleanor Leacock eds. New York: Praeger.

Thwaites, Reuben G., ed.
   1896 *The Jesuit Relations and Allied Documents.* 73 Vols. Cleveland: Burrows Brothers. [1896-1901].

Trigger, Bruce G.
   1978 Early Iroquoian Contacts with Europeans. Pp. 244-256 in *Handbook of North American Indians,* Vol. 15: Northeast. Bruce G. Trigger, ed. Washington: Smithsonian Institution.

Trowbridge, Charles C.
   1939 Shawnese Traditions. *University of Michigan Museum of Anthropology Occasional Contributions* 9. Vernon Kinietz and Ermine W. Voegelin, eds. Ann Arbor.

Voegelin, Charles F., and Ermine W.
   1944 The Shawnee Female Deity in Historical Perspective. *American Anthropologist* 46:370-375.

Weist, Kathryn B.
   1983 Beasts of Burden and Menial Slaves: Nineteenth Century Observations of Northern Plains Indian Women. In *The Hidden Half.* Patricia Albers, ed. Washington, D.C.: University Press of America.

Chapter 2:

The Shawnee Prophet and Handsome Lake

The Frontier Zone

The purpose of this paper is to compare and contrast the revitalization movements of Tenskwatawa (the Shawnee Prophet) and Handsome Lake of the Iroquois. Both of these revitalization movements took place within the context of a Frontier environment. Both the Shawnee and the Iroquois felt the effects of territorial expansion of the United States. Both the Shawnee and the Iroquois suffered from land loss, disease, depopulation and cultural disruption (cf. Howard 1981:1-23).

Hudson (1977:13) has stated that the term "Frontier" denotes not only territorial or geographic expansion but also "the notion that the Frontier is a peculiar type of society, and, moreover, that the movement of the Frontier zone is a kind of social process, not merely a series of isolines on a map." Thus the geographical expansion by the United States and the social process on the Frontier worked together in laying the foundation of conditions that allowed for the development of both the Shawnee and Iroquois revitalization movements.

Hudson notes that three essential variables can be used to identify a Frontier. These variables are time, location and population. For the purpose of this paper, the historical time frame is the late 18th and early 19th centuries (1799-1611). The locations involved are New York State and the Ohio Valley Region. The populations of concern are the Shawnee and Iroquois Indians.

There are other important factors that are essential in the study of a Frontier zone. These other factors include the environment, economy, culture and, most importantly, for the concerns of the present paper, the historical interactions between "the people, institutions, and environment on the edge of the settled territory" (Hudson 1977:22).

Acculturation and Revitalization

After coming into contact with the Europeans, both the Shawnee and Iroquois tribes began the process of acculturation. Berkhofer (1972:371) has deemed acculturation as "the process of interaction between two societies by which the culture of the society in subordinate position is drastically modified to conform to the culture of the dominant society."

One of the major agents of the acculturation process are missionaries. The missionaries played an important role in both the Shawnee and Iroquois revitalization movements because they provided the basis for the syncretic religion that was developed by both the Shawnee Prophet and Handsome Lake. The new syncretic religion was the core of both of these revitalization movements (cf. Deardorff 1951). Berkhofer (1972:373) has noted that in contrast to some other agents of the Frontier, the missionary "sought not only religious converts but the complete transformation of Indian Life."

Many anthropologists have done studies on Nativistic and revitalization movements. Linton (1943:238) has stated that a revivalist-magical type of Nativism may arise if a group incurs sufficient hardships. This type of movement occurs when the dominated group considers itself inferior as a result of European domination. This was true for both the Shawnee and the Iroquois. Linton makes several other important points regarding nativistic movements which will be illustrated by the two cases presented in this paper. Linton points out that it is quite easy to convert Nativistic movements into mechanisms for aggression. This will be illustrated by the Shawnee movement which began as a movement that was focused upon the religious teachings of the Shawnee Prophet and then was later converted into a mechanism of aggression to attempt to stop the geographical expansion of the United States. Linton also states that when a society is going through a revitalization movement, people within that society will react differently to it. This will also be illustrated by both the Shawnee and Iroquois cases:

In such societies, nativistic tendencies will be strongest in those classes of individuals who occupy a favored position and who feel this position threatened by culture change. This factor may produce a split in the society, the favored individuals or groups indulging in a rational Nativism, either revivalistic or perpetuative, while those in less favored positions are eager for assimilation. (Linton 1951:239)

Linton also notes that revivalistic movements function as a safety valve for the society and that in almost all Nativistic movements there is a situation of inequality between the two societies that come into contact

(Linton 1951:234). Both of these general statements are true for the Iroquois and Shawnee cases.

Although all types of Nativistic movements involve an attempt to revive extinct elements of a given culture, Linton defines several different types of Nativistic movements. The type under which both the Shawnee and Iroquois movements can be defined is the magical Nativistic type.

In a magical Nativistic movement, "some individual assumes the role of the prophet and is accepted by the people because they wish to believe. They always lean heavily on the supernatural and usually embody apocalyptic and millennial aspects" (Linton 1951:231). This general statement will also be illustrated by both the Shawnee and Iroquois cases.

Another anthropologist who has done extensive research on revitalization movements is Anthony F.C. Wallace. Wallace defines a revitalization movement "as a deliberate, organized, conscious effort by members of a society to construct a more satisfying culture" (Wallace 1956:265). Wallace has stated that all revitalization movements occur under two conditions: in situations of high individual stress, and in situations where a disillusionment with a distorted cultural Gestalt occurs (Wallace 1956:279). Wallace also points out that most revitalization movements are "conceived in a prophet's revelatory visions, which provide for him a satisfying relationship to the Supernatural and outline a new way of life under divine sanction."

Both the Shawnee and Iroquois revitalization movements illustrate the points expressed above by Wallace. In both Shawnee and Iroquois society there was disillusionment with a distorted cultural Gestalt and high individual stress. Handsome Lake and the Shawnee Prophet based their revitalization movement on revelatory visions.

The Shawnee

The Shawnee are an Algonquian-speaking tribal group that was so fragmented that "during their recorded history were never united into a single society" (Callender 1978:622). Due to their many migrations, the Shawnee came into contact with a variety of other tribes. Their most important associations were with the Iroquois, Delaware and the Creek.

Callender notes that the Shawnee contacts with the Iroquois were "very complex and shifted through several phases." Before European contact, the Iroquois drove the Shawnee out of the Ohio Valley. After the Shawnee had moved to Pennsylvania, the Iroquois treated the Shawnee as a subordinate group, and the exerted considerable influence over them.

The Delawares were neighbors of the Shawnee after the Shawnee settled in Eastern Pennsylvania. At times the two tribes even shared the same settlements. Later, both the Delaware and the Shawnee moved into the Ohio Valley. The Shawnee also had important contacts with the Creek. Callender stated: "The Shawnee connection with the Creek is far from adequately known, was apparently old and rather close, although limited in its extent. From the early post-contact period to the late 18th century, the Creek confederacy usually included at least one Shawnee town."

During the Fur trade period (the late 16th and early 17th centuries), the Shawnee had close contacts with the English who provided them with a market for their furs. The Shawnee also had trade contacts with the French. During this time period the Shawnee were involved in the "Colonial playoff system" between the English and the French. Throughout this period the Shawnee continually shifted their alliances in an effort to play off the Colonial powers against each other.

The Shawnee fought very hard to oppose trans-Appalachian settlement and they were involved in both Pontiac's rebellion and Lord Dunmore's war. The Shawnee were "probably the main force in the Indian coalition that resisted American expansion during and after the Revolution" (Callender 1978:623). Throughout this period the Shawnee suffered from land loss, fragmentation, warfare, disease, depopulation, a dwindling game supply and Anglo injustice. Edmunds (1983:5) noted that "the traditional failure of interpersonal relationships, formalized roles, and elaborate kinship groups came apart because the tribe was unable to cope with the rapid changes swirling around them.." All of these factors worked together to set the stage for the appearance of the Shawnee Prophet,

The Iroquois

The Iroquois were an Iroquoian-speaking tribe that resided in New York state. The League of the Iroquois consisted of five tribes: The Mohawk, Oneida, Onondaga, Cayuga and the Seneca. The Tuscarora tribe (from North Carolina) was allowed to join the League about 1722, but they never received full status and they really functioned in a subordinate position to the rest of the tribes.

The Iroquois were able to play off both the French and the British because of their strategic location:

> Iroquois neutrality, and the threat of its abandonment, thus
> became a lever by which Iroquois diplomats at endless rounds
> of treaties were able to extort courteous treatment, promises of

territorial integrity, large quantities of "presents" (which included guns, powder, lead, traps, cloth, kettles, knives, axes, awls, food and drink, and body ornaments), and favorable credit for Indian fur-trade hunters. (Wallace 1978:442)

Thus, before 1763, the Iroquois profited from contact with Europeans and "did not suffer directly from imperial domination."

After 1763, however, the situation for the Iroquois changed dramatically. Between 1763 and 1797 a series of military, political and economic disasters destroyed the equilibrium of the Iroquois cultural system. The first event that began this process was the British victory over the French in the French and Indian War. This put an abrupt end to the Colonial playoff system that the Iroquois had used so effectively to enhance their own position. The Iroquois' fortunes continued to decline after the failure of Pontiac's Rebellion. The material affluence of the Iroquois also declined due to a reduction of credit given to hunters, and because of a decrease in the amount of presents that they received from Anglos. At the Treaty of Ft. Stanwix in 1768, the Iroquois sold all of their land holdings south of the Ohio and west of the Alleghany mountains. This land sale ended the League's influence over the Shawnee, Delaware and the Wyandots who resided in the Ohio Valley region (Wallace 1978:443).

During the American Revolution, the Iroquois fought on the side of the British, and, although they inflicted considerable damage to the American Frontier, their towns were devastated by the 1778 expedition of John Sullivan. The Sullivan expedition burned houses and crops in almost every Iroquois town. After the Sullivan expedition, the surviving Iroquois sought refuge at Fort Niagara. The condition of the Iroquois at Fort Niagara was deplorable. The Iroquois at Fort Niagara were underfed, inadequately sheltered and suffered from epidemic disease. By the end of the Revolutionary War, the Iroquois had suffered from, massive depopulation, their numbers reduced to only half their former size (Wallace 1978:443).

From 1783 to 1797, the Iroquois signed away almost all of their remaining land holdings at the Fort Stanwix and Big Tree Treaties (Tooker 1978:434-435). The Iroquois had entered the reservation period. Thus, in summary, after 1763, the Iroquois suffered from rapid depopulation, loss of their land base, increased factionalism, increased use of alcohol and loss of their military and diplomatic power. At the start of the reservation period, the Iroquois also suffered from a lack of leadership. Their traditional religious rituals had also declined in importance which resulted in further fragmentation of Iroquois society. Clearly by 1797, the Iroquois culture was in dire need of revitalization (cf. Deardorff 1951:83, 84).

The Shawnee Prophet

There is some dispute regarding the birth date of the Shawnee Prophet. Some sources state that the Prophet (Lalawethika) was born in 1768 (Howard 1981:198), while other sources state that he was born in 1775 (Edmunds 1983:29). Before the Prophet received his first revelation, his name was Lalawethika ('Rattle'). After receiving his first vision, he changed his name to Tenskwatawa ('The Open Door[1]). Lalawethika's father, Puckeshinwa, was a chief of the Kispotha division. His mother, Methoataske ("Turtle Laying Its Eggs') may have been of Creek descent, but here again, the sources do not agree.

Before Lalawethika was born, his father was killed at the Battle of Point Pleasant. Another disagreement in the sources centers on the age of Lalawethika's brother Tecumseh. Howard stated that Lalawethika and his brother Tecumseh were born in the Shawnee village of Piqua which was located on the Mad River. Howard's informant, Ranny Carpenter, told him that there were three brothers, the third brother having a narrow, deformed head (Howard 1981:198). Howard's assertion is also supported by one of Radin's informants (Radin 1970:71). This third brother died within a year. Shortly after giving birth, Methodtoske abandoned her children. It is unclear what happened to her although it is speculated that she may have returned to the Creeks or joined the Kipppkothas who left Ohio in 1779.

There is another disagreement in the sources concerning Tecumseh's age. Howard states that Tecumseh was the same age as Lalawethika, while Edmunds states that Tecumseh was seven years older than Lalawethika, although he does state that the Prophet was born as a triplet (Howard 1981:197), Although part of the problem with these conflicts in the sources may be due to problems inherent with work in oral history, it is not the purpose of this paper to attempt to resolve these conflicting statements.

Thus Lalawethika and his brother were left without parents. Tecumpease (Lalawethika's older married sister) raised the boys. Tecumpease and her husband Wasabagoa ('Stand Firm') did their best to raise the boys. A war chief named Black Fish also took an interest in the boys. Edmunds (1983:30) stated that "Tecumpease and her husband, Wasabagoa ("Stand Firm"), favored Tecumseh over either of the younger brothers and although the Shawnee woman spent hours with Tecumseh, she generally ignored Lalawethika."

Lalawethika had a very difficult childhood. He was not handsome and was rather fat. As a result he did not excel at childhood games that other Shawnee boys played. Lalawethika was frustrated by this and, to compensate for his failures, he became a braggart (Edmunds 1983:72).

Lalawethika's older brother, Chiksika, avoided his younger brother, and, as a result, Lalawethika did not receive proper training and was a poor hunter. Later, Lalawethika blinded his right eye with an arrow. As an adolescent, Lalawethika began to drink quite heavily and as a result his behaviour became even worse causing him to alienate his already small group of family and friends (Edmunds 1978:74).

When Lalawethika reached his mid-20s, his hunting skills were still so poor that he had to rely upon his friends and relatives to provide meat for his family. Due to his incompetence as a hunter, Lalawethika was the laughing-stock of the village and began to drink even more heavily than before. Forsyth had this to say regarding Lalawethika: "When a boy he was a perfect vagabond and as he grew up he became a great drunkard." (Forsyth 1912:274).

Lalawethika then began to associate himself with a Shaman named Penagashla. Although the Shaman disliked Lalawethika, he eventually instructed the young Shawnee in herbs, healing and incantations. When Penagashla died in 1804, Lalawethika attempted to take his place, but tribal distrust and an epidemic caused him to fail. In 1805, an epidemic struck the village resulting in the death of several Shawnees. This incident proved that Lalawethika was not a good Shaman, and his credibility as a healer became non-existent. After this event, Lalawethika withdrew to his wigwan in disappointment (Edmunds 1978:75).

Handsome Lake

Handsome Lake was a half-brother of Cornplanter and a member of the Alleghany band who lived on a 42-mile tract of land along the Alleghany River. Some of the Alleghany band also lived on the Cornplanter grant, which Cornplanter had received as a reward for his cooperation in a variety of treaties. The land itself was a gift from the Commonwealth of Pennsylvania.

Handsome Lake lived with Cornplanter. In the spring of 1799, just a few months before Handsome Lake received his first vision, the Alleghany band was suffering from a variety of problems that were common for many American Indian tribes during the reservation period. During the spring of 1799 there were drunken brawls and accusations of witchcraft. This witchcraft outbreak came to a climax with the execution of a witch who was accused of causing the death of a niece of Cornplanter and Handsome Lake.

For Handsome Lake the death of his niece only added to his problems. During the spring of 1799 he lay on his bunk "bound in sickness by some strong power and pondered the cause of his illness and the disturbed state of his people" (Wallace 1972:239). Handsome Lake's illness was probably related to his excessive drinking habits. In short, Wallace stated that Handsome Lake was "suffering from the classic Iroquois bereavement syndrome compacted of depression, bitterness, and suspicion" (Wallace 1972:240).

Application of a Model of the Prophetic Process

This section of the paper will involve the application of Overholt's model of the prophetic process to both the Shawnee Prophet's and Handsome Lake's revitalization movement.

Overholt's model is concerned with the dynamics of the prophetic act itself. He defines the prophetic process "as one of reciprocal interaction and adjustment between a minimum of three distinct actors or groups: the supernatural, the prophet, and the people to whom the prophet's message is addressed" (Overholt 1975:38). Overholt also notes that every prophet is influenced by his own historical-cultural context, and that this in turn influences the dynamics of the prophet's movement.

The supernatural element is obviously an abstraction, since it is impossible for a person to observe it directly. The prophet must use sensory reality to represent the supernatural to his audience. The prophet functions to convey the abstract supernatural to his people by providing them with verbal descriptions of the supernatural world that was revealed to him during his vision. This descriptive act almost always occurs in a public forum atmosphere where the people question the prophet about the supernatural world that has been revealed to him through his vision.

The prophet thus serves as a messenger to the people whose authority is based on two things: his revelations, and his acceptance by his people. After the prophet has revealed his message to the people, the people respond. The people will then put the prophet's message to the test "by deciding whether or not it is in continuity with the broad cultural tradition and congruous with the current socio-political situation" (Overholt 1975:38). Each member of the prophet's community will react somewhat differently to the prophet's message. Dissent to a prophet's message can come in two forms: feedback and outright rejection. After the prophet communicates his message to his people and they respond to it, feedback results. Feedback from the people then results in an alteration of the prophet's original message. Both the Shawnee Prophet and Handsome Lake changed their original messages as a result of feedback from the people.

Overholt (1975:39-40) gives the following set of test implications for his model of the prophetic process:

1. The prophet's revelation.
2. Characteristics of the prophet's message.
   a. Cultural continuity.
   b. Cognizance of the current historical context.
   c. External influences upon the message.
3. Feedback from the people will come in the form of:
   a. Action.
   b. A set of expectations.
4. Prophetic feedback to the source of the revelation.
5. Additional revelation(s).
6. Additional message(s).
7. Adjustment of expectations on the part of the auditors.
8. The work of disciples.

The Shawnee Prophet's First Revelation

In early 1805 Lalawethika experienced his first revelation. His wife found him lying face down in their lodge, and when she spoke to him he did not respond. Lalawethika's eyes were closed and he did not appear to be breathing. Thinking that Lalawethika had died, his wife and neighbors began to make funeral preparations; but before the arrangements could be completed Lalawethika awakened to tell of his revelation from the Master of Life. Mooney gave the following account of the Prophet's first revelation:

One day, while lighting his pipe in his cabin he fell back apparently lifeless and remained in that condition until his friends had assembled for the funeral when he revived from his trance, quieted their alarm, and announced that he had been conducted to the spirit world. In November 1805, when hardly more than 30 years of age, he called around his tribesmen and their allies at their ancient capital of Wapakonela within the present limits of Ohio, and announced himself as the bearer of a new revelation from the Master of Life. He declared that he had been taken up to the spirit world and had been permitted to lift the well of the past and the future, had seen the misery of evil-doers and learned the happiness that awaited those who followed the precepts of the Indian god. He then began an earnest exhortation, denouncing the witchcraft and medicine juggleries of the tribe, and solemnly warning his hearers that none who had part in such things would ever taste of the future happiness. (Mooney 1896:729)

Edmunds (1983:33) also provides an account of the key elements of the prophet's first revelation. He states that during his revelation, the prophet was shown both the future and the past. The prophet also saw paradise that was rich in game and fine corn fields. This was a place "where the spirits of virtuous Shawnees could flourish and continue the same type of life in paradise that they enjoyed on earth." The Shawnee Prophet was also shown a large lodge which the sinful tribesmen were forced to enter. Inside the lodge an enormous fire burned and "the sinners were subjected to a fiery torture in accordance with their wickedness." The souls of these sinful tribesmen could not enter heaven until they had atoned for their sins, and even after they were allowed to enter paradise they still could not share in all the pleasures that the more virtuous tribesmen enjoyed. These scenes from the prophet's first revelation show clear influences from Christianity and illustrate that the prophet had incorporated several features borrowed from Christianity with elements of traditional Shawnee religion and developed a true syncretic religion.

Handsome Lake's First Revelation

In June of 1799, Handsome Lake collapsed outside his cabin. His daughter called his nephew Blacksnake for assistance. Handsome Lake appeared dead but was actually only in a trance state in which he received his first revelation from the Creator.

During his vision, Handsome Lake was visited by three middle-aged men (angels) who were dressed in fine ceremonial clothing. The angels informed Handsome Lake that he had earned the right to get help to recover from his illness because of his constant thankfulness. Handsome Lake was told to join his people at the Strawberry Festival and "report what the Creator had to say about how things should be on earth" (Wallace 1972:241). Handsome Lake was instructed to inform his people to continue to hold the annual festival. He was also told to inform his people that whiskey, witchcraft, love magic and abortion-and-sterility medicine were evil and that all of these things displeased the Creator. Handsome Lake was also instructed to tell his people that individuals who were found guilty of these wrongs must confess their sins and vow not to sin again. Moderate sinners were allowed to confess their sins in private to Handsome Lake, but more wicked sinners had to "confess alone to the Creator." The angels excused Handsome Lake for his sins of intoxication saying that his suffering had excused him. They told him that he must never drink again, not even in private, and informed him that they would return.

Thus Handsome Lake's first revelation centered upon confession. Wallace has noted that his first vision was essentially apocalyptic in nature and was concerned with the themes of sin, damnation and the destruction of the world. The practices of drinking, magic and witchcraft were condemned, and people were urged to confess their sins so that they could achieve salvation. After receiving his first vision, Handsome Lake requested that his brother call his people to council and inform them of Handsome Lake's vision. When Handsome Lake related his vision to the people it had a "profound effect on the assembled audience" (Wallace 1972:242).

Thus Handsome Lake's vision and the Shawnee Prophet's vision were remarkably similar. Both of them condemned drinking and stressed the need for the confession of sins. Strong apocalyptic themes were present in both revelations, and both of their visions illustrate the influence of contact with Christianity. In short, both of these prophets combined traditional elements of their culture with new features that were borrowed from Christianity and wove them into a new syncretic religion that was better adapted to fit the requirements of the historical context in which they first appeared.

The Shawnee Prophet's Message

It is clear that the Shawnee Prophet's essential message was obtained from his first revelation. H.R. Schoolcraft indicated the general features of the prophet's message: He told the Indians that their pristine state, antecedent to the arrival of the Europeans, was most agreeable to the Great Spirit, and that they had adopted too many manners and customs of the Whites. He counseled them to return to their primeval simple condition; to throw away their flints and steels, and to resort to their original mode of obtaining fire by percussion. He denounced the woolen gifts as not equal to skins for clothing; he commended the use of the bow and arrow . . . (Schoolcraft 1854:354)

In a letter to General William Clark dated December 23, 1812, Thomas Forsyth (1912) provided a list of as many of the laws of the Shawnee Prophet as he could recall. These laws can be summarized as follows:

1. All drinking was forbidden.
2. Monogamy was to be the rule in the future.
3. Although a husband did have a right to beat his wife if she behaved poorly or neglected her duties, after the punishment was over the couple were to forgive each other and bear no ill toward each other.
4. Indian women who resided with Whites were to return.
5. All medicine bags, dances and songs were to be destroyed. The medicine had to be destroyed in the presence of the entire tribe and had to be accompanied by a personal confession in which the person told of his or her bad deeds and asked the Great Spirit for forgiveness.
6. Indians were forbidden to sell provisions to Whites.
7. Indians could not eat any food that was cooked by a white person, nor could they eat any provisions raised by Whites.
8. Indians were not allowed to sell skins or furs. They could only exchange these goods for other articles.
9. Although the French, English and Spaniards could be considered as friends, Indians were warned to stay away from Americans.
10. Articles of Anglo clothing (like hats) were to be given back. Cats and dogs were also supposed to be returned.
11. Indians were to refrain from purchasing merchandise. The Prophet stated that this would encourage the game to become plentiful again so that the Indians would no longer be economically dependent upon the Whites.
12. All Indians who refused to follow these laws were considered to be evil and
    would be put to death.
13. The Shawnee Prophet instructed the Indians to be faithful in their prayers.

Tenskwatawa told his followers that if they followed his laws faithfully that in four years' time two days of darkness would occur. During this time "the Creator would travel invisibly throughout the land, and cause the animals that had been created to come forth again out of the earth" (Howard 1981:203). The Prophet also promised his followers that their dead friends would come back to life. The Shawnee Prophet's first revelation was clearly apocalyptic.

Handsome Lake's Message

Handsome Lake's message, which was based on his first revelation, centered upon several themes. Handsome Lake urged his people to continue to hold the annual Strawberry Festival- Like the Shawnee Prophet, an important part of Handsome Lake's message was the concern with the act of confession. People could confess their sins in public or in private, depending upon the extent of their wickedness. Handsome Lake also forbid whiskey, witchcraft, love magic and abortion-and-sterility medicine. All of these things were evil and they displeased the Creator (Wallace 1972:239-241).

The Shawnee Prophet's Feedback

The Shawnee Prophet's teachings spread quite rapidly in the first several months after his first revelation, and within a short period of time his message had been received by several tribes. These tribes included the Pottowatomis, the Ottawas, the Wyandots, the Chippewas, Menominies, Winnebagos, Sacs and Delawares.

Edmunds notes that the Prophet's message spread rapidly among the Delawares. Some of the Delawares traveled to Greenville to meet with the Prophet. After they returned to their own villages, they enlisted many converts to the Prophet's doctrines. The Delawares were very concerned with the Prophet's admonitions concerning witchcraft, and "searching within their society, they probed for those who appeared to be servants of the Evil Spirit" (Edmunds 1983:42). The Delaware witch hunt resulted in the death of five people, all of whom were burned at the stake (Edmunds 1983:42-46).

John Tanner's narrative on the Ottawa and Ojibwa provides us with some conception of how great the effects of the Shawnee Prophet's teachings could be on a particular tribe. Tanner stated the enthusiasm for the Prophet's doctrines was so great that even he threw away his medicine bag and flint and steel. He stated that "the influence of the Shawnee Prophet was very sensibly and painfully felt by the remotest Ojibbewas of whom I had any knowledge" (Tanner 1830:147). (Other writers have noted that the Prophet's teachings had very similar effects upon other tribes.)

Although space consideration does not allow for a discussion of the feedback reactions from all the tribes that were involved with the Shawnee Prophet's movement, this is not to suggest that all of the feedback was of a positive nature. In general, the people who reacted most negatively to the Prophet's teachings were the ones who had the most to lose; especially the tribal chiefs and Shamans who were the most threatened by the Prophet's doctrines. The laws that met with the strongest opposition were the Prophet's proscription of medicine bags, medicine rites and dogs.

In the summer of 1806, Tenskwatawa greatly increased his credibility with an accurate prediction of an eclipse: By some means he had learned that an eclipse of the sun was to take place in the summer of 1806. As the time drew near, he called about him the scoffers and boldly announced that on a certain day he would prove to him his supernatural authority by causing the sun to become dark. When the day and hour arrived and the earth at mid-day was enveloped in the gloom of twilight, Tenskwatawa, standing in the midst of the terrified Indians, pointed to the sky and cried, "Did I not speak the truth? See the sun is dark!" There were no more doubters now. All proclaimed him a true Prophet and the messenger of the Master of Life. His fame spread abroad and apostles began to carry his revelations to the remotest tribes. (Mooney 1890:674)

Handsome Lake's Feedback

Like the Shawnee Prophet, Handsome Lake received both positive and negative feedback from his people concerning his doctrines. Jackson (1830:42-45) stated that during the years of 1800-1802, Handsome Lake had acquired considerable influence over the nation. He also noted that although some of the younger men were somewhat dissatisfied, his popularity was still quite high.

Handsome Lake's cause was helped by an official endorsement of support that he received from President Thomas Jefferson. Jefferson advised the Indians "to open your ears to the council of Handsome Lake, to listen to his advice and to be governed by his precepts" (Deardorff 1951:94). The President's support helped to put Handsome Lake beyond reach of the faction that opposed him.

The heaviest opposition to the Iroquois Prophet came from Buffalo Creek while the Prophet had very strong support at Coldspring. Handsome Lake, like the Shawnee Prophet, also went on a witch hunt for a period of time. Several Indians were killed on charges of witchcraft. Handsome Lake met with the strongest opposition to his doctrines on witchcraft and his law against schooling for Indian children. Even Cornplanter did not agree with these two points of his doctrine. Due to strong opposition on these issues, Handsome Lake later revised his position on schooling and discontinued his witch hunt.

The Prophet's Feedback to the Supernatural

This part of Overholt's model of the dynamics of the prophetic process is rather abstract. Overholt (1975:48) states that the assumption here is "that, since the prophet understands himself as a messenger of the supernatural, he will depend on further revelations for developments and/or changes in his message." The Prophet also takes into account the negative feedback that he receives from the people, and, based on that, he revises or changes elements of his original doctrine. The Prophet then gives the people his new message with the modifications already added in. All of these changes receive sanction from the supernatural. Thus, through this process, the Prophet adapts and changes his message to better suit the current circumstances.

The elements of his original message that the Shawnee Prophet fed back to the Supernatural were the points of his doctrine which caused the most factionalism. Tenskwatawa discontinued his witch hunt because of the great factionalism it created. He reversed his former position against the sale of goods and skins to Anglos. He also recalled his laws against eating food cooked by White people as well as his law against purchasing merchandise from Anglos. Tenskwatawa changed these points of his doctrine because of the factionalism that some of them had created and for practical reasons (for example: the requirements of food) (Edmunds 1983:76).

Handsome Lake's Feedback to the Supernatural

Handsome Lake also fed back some of the points of his original doctrine to the Supernatural because of the opposition that some of these doctrines had caused. The first thing he discontinued was his witch hunt; he also revised his former position on farming and education for Indians. Due to strong opposition, Handsome Lake made accommodations on both of these issues.

Handsome Lake's new position on farming was that Indians could learn how to farm so long as they did not sell the excess crops for profit, but gave them to the poor. On the subject of education for Indians he said that "although reading and writing are not good for Indians, even it is well that some of your children learn so that they may deal with the Whites for you" (Deardorff 1951:103).

Additional Revelations by Prophets

Both the Shawnee Prophet and Handsome Lake received additional revelations. Some of their essential doctrines and messages stayed fairly constant over time. Other specific points of their doctrines changed over time in response to feedback from the people. Thus, on some points, both Prophets just amplified their original message, while on other issues changes did occur (Overholt 1975:49).

Additional Revelations of the Shawnee Prophet

After he had received his first revelation, the Shawnee Prophet continued to experience visions. Edmunds (1883:34) states that "Tenskwatawa experienced additional visions and enlarged on his doctrines of Indian deliverance." One of Tenskwatawa's additional revelations was described by a Winnebago informant of Paul Radin. The first part of the account centers upon the fact that at first Tenskwatawa was misled by the Devil and did not set out to do the task of prophecy that the Creator had instructed him to do. One day, when the Shawnee Prophet was bathing, a man came to him and gave him the following message: "They have told me to come after you, so let us go." Then he went back with him and he took him to the place from which he had originally started (the other world, our Grandmother's home). Then the Creator said, "How are you getting on with the work which you were to do?" Then he remembered what he had been doing. Then the Creator said, "Is it for this that I created you?" Then he took his mouth and showed it to him and he saw that it was crooked and sticking out in all directions. Then he took his understanding (and showing it to him) he said, "Did I create you thus?" Then he looked into his ears and they were crooked and ragged. Thus he made him see all his bad characteristics and his evil mind. Then he took out his heart and showed it to him. It was all furrowed up and bad to look upon. "Did I create you thus?" said the creator. (Howard 1983:200)

Handsome Lake's Additional Revelations:
The Sky Journey

Several weeks after receiving his first revelation, Handsome Lake fell into a trance. It was during this trance state that Handsome Lake had his sky journey vision. During this journey, Handsome Lake was led across heaven and hell by a guide and was given the "moral plan of the cosmos" (Wallace 1972:246). Before the guide left Handsome Lake, he praised him for telling his people of his vision and again reminded Handsome Lake of the evils of alcohol and witchcraft. The guide also told Handsome Lake that the people must not confuse dreams inspired by the Devil with those inspired by the Great Spirit. The guide also warned Handsome Lake that "unless the people mended their ways, thought more about the Great Spirit, and immediately conducted the White Dog ceremony, a great sickness would come upon the village."

Handsome Lake had his third vision on February 5, 1800. The essential message of this vision was that the Great Spirit was "still very concerned over the condition of the Indians" (Wallace 1972:246). In this vision, three angels again expressed their concern over the evils of witchcraft and whiskey. The angels told Handsome Lake that he should write down his revelations so that the Indians could always remember them. The angels also stressed that the children were to be raised in the teachings of the Gaiwio. They also told Handsome Lake that the Iroquois must continue to practice their traditional rituals, especially the Midwinter ceremony. After Handsome Lake had received his third vision, his apocalyptic gospel was completed. Wallace (1978:446-447) stated that this apocalyptic gospel "contained three major, interrelated themes: the imminence of world destruction; the definition of sin; and the prescription for salvation."

The Shawnee Prophet's Additional Messages

Many of the Shawnee Prophet's additional messages were simply a restatement of his essential doctrine of laws that he had already given. The Shawnee Prophet continued to stress the elimination of alcohol, medicine bundles and various items of Anglo clothing. He also warned the Indians about, the evils of sexual promiscuity, violence, Anglo technology and the accumulation of personal property and material wealth. The Prophet told people to keep their fires burning in their lodges stating that "if you suffer your fire to be extinguished, at that moment your life will be at its end" (Edmunds 1983:36). Although the Shawnee Prophet stated that some of the traditional Shawnee dances were corrupt, he "suggested new ones that would please both the Master of Life and bring joy to the dancers." The Prophet's religion contained elaborate rituals. Kendall (1809:292) states that he observed one ceremonial that "involved the men dancing naked with their bodies painted, and with war clubs in their hands." Howard (1981) has pointed out that Kendall's description seems to apply to the men's ceremonial war dance which is still performed by the Absentee Shawnee.

The Shawnee Prophet also had to change or modify some of his original doctrines in response to both internal and external pressures. For example, although the Prophet had been told by the Master of Life that Greenville was the proper site for him to teach his doctrines, the Prophet decided to move from this location, The Prophet decided to move because of practical reasons; not because of any new supernatural revelations. The

Greenville location was too close to the Anglo frontier, thus it was very vulnerable to attack. The Prophet also moved the village because he had experienced strong opposition from some local federal Indian agents and other Indians near the Greenville site (Edmunds 1983:68). A shortage of food also caused the Prophet to revise some of his doctrines. Although in his original doctrine the Prophet stated that no Indian was to eat any provisions raised by Anglos, Tenskawatawa changed this rule because the Indians at Prophetstown were starving. Edmunds (1963:69) notes that "Although the Master of Life frowned on such sustenance, during February and March the Prophet and his people slaughtered stray hogs and cattle they found wandering in the nearby forest." Thus the Shawnee Prophet was constantly changing his message in response to both internal and external forces.

Handsome Lake's Additional Messages

All of the additional messages that Handsome Lake gave to his people were based on additional revelations. Handsome Lake continued to preach against whiskey and magic. He also continued to instruct people in the importance of confession. Both of these doctrines were based on Handsome Lake's first revelation. Handsome Lake also urged that all the Iroquois children should be raised in accordance with the teachings of Gawio ('Good Message'). Handsome Lake stressed that the traditional ceremonies must be continued, especially the Midwinter ceremony. Although Handsome Lake urged the people to continue to practice the traditional ceremonies, he did ask for some ritual changes in the traditional Iroquoian ceremonial system.

Handsome Lake condemned the Iroquois medicine societies. He also called for the elimination of the anniversary mourning ceremonies. Handsome Lake added the concept of a heaven and hell (with the idea of divine judgment) to the Iroquois religion. This innovation was not hard to accept, however, because of the traditional duality belief in the good and evil twins.'

Like the Shawnee Prophet, Handsome Lake had to modify, or change some of his doctrines in response to both internal and external sources of conflict. Handsome Lake eventually abandoned his witch hunt due to strong opposition from both Indians (including his own brother Cornplanter), and because of pressure from Anglos (primarily the Quakers),

Deardorff (1951:101) has noted that Handsome Lake's message was very adaptable. He also notes that although Handsome Lake was originally opposed to the Quakers on some parts of his doctrine, it was not very long before he began to make some accommodations. In response to pressure from the Quakers, Handsome Lake changed his stance on farming and education. Although Handsome Lake had originally said that Indians should not farm in the Anglo style to grow a surplus, he later changed his mind on this matter, saying that it was alright for the Indians to learn the Anglo method of farming, but only if they gave their surplus to the needy and did not sell it for profit. Although he was originally opposed to Indian education, he changed this point of his doctrine stating that although reading and writing are not good for Indians, it is good to have some of the children learn these skills so that they can deal with the Anglos. All of these accommodations by Handsome Lake allowed his doctrine to remain flexible to meet changing circumstances. Deardorff provides a good summation of this point:

> Handsome Lake's function seems to have been to select and prune a strong native stock and to encourage grafting good scions thereon, leaving each gardener to determine pretty much for himself what is "good" since the "bad" will not survive anyhow. The Quakers had taught him how to do it. (Deardorff 1951:103)

Adjustment of Expectations: Shawnee Prophet

As the Shawnee Prophet continued to communicate his messages, the people (or his auditors) changed their expectations of the Prophet. For example, fairly early in the movement the auditors had to adjust their expectations about the Shawnee Prophet because the expected millennium did not occur at the end of four years as the prophet had predicted. This undoubtedly caused some of the prophet's followers to become a bit skeptical.

The realities of a harsh winter at Prophetstown also cast doubt upon the prophet. The tribes at Prophetstown were starving and they also suffered from disease. Although this sickness seemed to pass over the Shawnees, Kickapoos and Wyandots, almost 160 Ottawas and Chippewas died, as a result of which the Ottawas and Chippewas began to doubt the Prophet's divinity. They began to think that perhaps he was a false prophet or that he might have poisoned his victims. The Ottawas and Chippewas decided to put the prophet to the test. Earlier, the prophet had warned his followers that if there was any violence committed in his village the "master of Life would destroy the perpetrators" (Edmunds 1983:77).

In April of 1809, a war party of Ottawas and Chippewas killed a Shawnee woman and child at Prophetstown and then fled back to their temporary camp. "When no great calamity befell them they rode confidently back to Michigan, spreading the world of Tenskwatawa's vulnerability. On their return, warriors from several villages of Ottawas and Chippewas assembled, making plans to attack the Prophet's village" (Edmunds 1983:77). The Shawnee Prophet tried to explain these deaths by stating that the woman and her child had died from natural causes (i.e., from Anglo diseases), and that the war party had only butchered the corpses. Tenskwatawa also tried to obtain warriors from the Sacs, Kickapoos and the Potowatomi's to protect his village from attack. Tenskwatawa also received some unexpected help from Governor William Hull who sent messages to both the Chippewas and the Ottawas forbidding them to attack the Shawnees.

Tenskwatawa's fatal mistake came shortly before the Battle of Tippacanoe when he assured his warriors of a victory over the Americans. Tenskwatawa assured his followers that the Master of Life had given him the medicine that would provide them with a victory over the Americans. He told his warriors that they would be invulnerable to the Americans: He would send rain and hail to dampen the Americans' powder, but the weapons of his warriors would not be affected. His followers must strike the Long Knives before dawn, for in the darkness his medicine would spread confusion to the American ranks and they would fall to the ground in a stupor. The same darkness would hide the warriors and blind the soldiers, while he would provide light "like the noon-tide sun" to guide the Indians. But Tenskwatawa warned the warriors that they must kill Harrison. The Master of Life had demanded that the Governor should die, for if he lived, the Long Knives could never be defeated. When Harrison fell, the surviving soldiers "would run and hide in the grass like young quails". Then they could be captured and forced to serve as slaves for the women of Prophetstown. (Edmunds 1983:110-111)

After the Indians lost the Battle of Tippacanoe, some of the tribesmen wanted to kill Tenskwatawa for misleading them. Although Tenskwatawa tried to blame his failure on his wife, whom he said had touched sacred objects while she was having her menstrual cycle, thus causing his medicine not to work, his attempt failed. After this event, almost all his followers left Prophetstown, and the era of influence of the Shawnee Prophet came to an end. He had made the same fatal mistake as many other Indian prophets. He had tied his success to military victories, at best a very risky business to engage in

Adjustment of Expectations: Handsome Lake

Handsome Lake's followers also had to make some adjustments of their expectations. Handsome Lake's followers, like those of the Shawnee Prophet had to adjust to an expected millennium that did not take place. Almost all of the adjustments of expectations that took place were ones that were required because of the changes in Iroquois society that Handsome Lake made through the introduction of some of his doctrines. The most important adjustments were ones based on reforms and changes that Handsome Lake introduced through his social gospel.

There were some fundamental changes as well as some new introductions to Iroquois society that Handsome Lake introduced through his social gospel. Handsome Lake favoured both Anglo-style farming and education. Both of these things required adjustments by the Iroquois. Individual Iroquois had to change their views on the role of men in agriculture, because in traditional Iroquois society, women were the primary agricultural workers. With the push for Angio-style farming, which is based on the principal that the males functioned as the primary agricultural workers, traditional Iroquois had to change their orientation of the division of labour in society between the sexes.

Another change that Handsome Lake stressed was the importance of the nuclear family. In traditional Iroquois culture the maternal lineage was more important than the nuclear family. Thus the Iroquois had to adjust their perspective on the importance of various kin ties. Handsome Lake also favoured material acculturation and accommodation with the Anglos, although he did resist any further loss of Indian lands.

Handsome Lake's followers also had to adjust to some new features that Handsome Lake added to their religion. The most important new features were the important of acts of confession, the introduction of a High God and the introduction of heaven and hell (future reward and punishment). All of these things show influence from Christianity and illustrate that Handsome Lake's reforms resulted in a new syncretic form of Iroquois religion that blended traditional elements with some new features borrowed from contact with Christianity. It is important to note however, as Wallace has pointed out, that Handsome Lake's High God may have not been intended to replace, but merely complement the earlier deity. Not all of these changes required drastic alterations of traditional forms. For example, the addition of the notion of a heaven and hell and future reward and punishment fit in very well with the traditional dualistic conflict in Iroquois society between the good and evil twins (Morrison and Ezzo 1985:142)

Conclusion

In concluding this cross-cultural study of the revitalization movements of Tenskwatawa (the Shawnee Prophet) and Handsome Lake, I would first like to summarize the essential points of the paper. First, it has been shown that both of these movements took place within the context of a Frontier environment. During the 18th Century, both the Iroquois and the Shawnee felt the effects of external influences from the American Frontier. The Shawnee and Iroquois felt the effects of geographical expansion by the United States as well as a variety of social processes which laid the foundation for both of these revitalization movements. Both the Shawnee and the Iroquois were in an inferior position compared to the advancing American Frontier. Due to this position of inferiority, both of these tribes suffered from numerous hardships including: land loss, fragmentation, warfare, disease and depopulation. In response to these conditions, both the Iroquois and the Shawnee began a revivalist magical type of Nativism under the leadership of a prophet. Both Handsome Lake and the Shawnee Prophet attempted to organize a conscious group effort to revitalize their culture. Both prophets leaned very heavily on the Supernatural and their movements embodied both apocalyptic and millennial themes. Both based their movements on revelatory visions or revelations from the Supernatural which were obtained while the prophet was in an altered state of consciousness. It should also be pointed out that both Handsome Lake and the Shawnee Prophet were in a very disadvantageous social position in their society before they received their first revelations. It seems highly probable that both used their revelations to elevate themselves to a higher social position (Henry 1982:396). Both of these prophets seem to have experienced what Prince (1982:418) calls "the omnipotence manoeuver". Prince states that this manoeuver can occur in circumstances of high life stress, near-death experiences and from artificially induced hyperstress. This feeling of euphoria that is experienced "is commonly linked with the idea of supernatural intervention." Clearly both Handsome Lake and the Shawnee Prophet seemed to have experienced the "omnipotence manoeuver".

Overholts's model of the prophetic process was applied to both these two revitalization movements. This dynamic model is based upon the interactions of the Supernatural, the Prophet and the people. Both of these Prophets were influenced by both internal forces (other tribe members) and external forces (opposing chiefs, Indian agents, missionaries and government officials). Overholt's model was tested by using a set of test implications. These test implications include: the prophet's revelation, characteristics of the prophet's message, feedback from the people, feedback to the supernatural, additional revelations, additional messages, and the adjustment of expectations (Overholt 1975:39-40). This model has proved very applicable to both of these revitalization movements. All of the stages of Overholt's model of prophet dynamics appear in both Handsome Lake's and the Shawnee Prophet's movement. Not only is Overholt's model applicable to both of these movements, it also illustrates that in many ways, the revitalization movements of Handsome Lake and the Shawnee Prophet were remarkably similar.

Both Handsome Lake and the Shawnee Prophet attempted to revitalize their culture by stressing some elements of the traditional culture and by adding new elements of Anglo culture. Both Handsome Lake and the Shawnee Prophet also condemned those items which they saw as threatening to their traditional society (intoxicants, private property ownership, certain material goods). Both of these prophets developed a syncretic religion which mixed traditional religious doctrines with some new features that were borrowed from Christianity, including the notion of confession, future reward and punishment, and the existence of a High God.

The main difference between these two revitalization movements is to be found in their degree of adaptability, accommodation and aggression. The Shawnee Prophet made the fatal mistake of trying to use his movement as a vehicle for aggression against the dominant Anglo culture. His fatal mistake was his prediction of the Indians military success at the Battle of Tippacanoe. The loss of this battle marked the end of his revitalization movement.

Handsome Lake did not attempt to convert his movement into a vehicle for aggression. He allowed his doctrines to remain very flexible and adapted and changed them over many times to meet new requirements of forced acculturation by Anglo society. Not only was Handsome Lake's doctrine more flexible than the Shawnee Prophet's, he also introduced a number of changes in Iroquois society that enabled the Iroquois to adapt to conditions that were present in the early 19th Century at the start of the reservation period. His most fundamental changes were reforms in agriculture and the Iroquoian family. Although Handsome Lake stressed the importance of traditional rituals, he also favoured material acculturation and accommodation with the larger Anglo society. Handsome Lake was also very successful in creating a very strong syncretic Iroquois religion that was very well adapted to the historical context in which it appeared. This new religion revitalized Iroquois culture. All of these changes which Handsome Lake introduced as part of his social gospel were adaptations that allowed the Iroquois to revitalize their traditional culture as well as make the necessary accommodations that were required by the Anglo society with the start of the reservation period.

The fact that the religion of Handsome Lake is still followed by Iroquois today illustrates how successful his revitalization movement was. Wallace sums it up well, noting that Handsome Lake's movement:

> provided effective moral sanction for certain moral, technological, and social adaptations that the Iroquois had to make if they were to survive at all. More generally, it can be seen as having not only made possible the adoption of survival techniques, but also enabled Iroquois people to do this in a time of crisis without losing contact with their past and without sacrificing their identity and self-respect as Indians, and to the present time, it has played an important part in the preservation of Iroquois cultural heritage. (Wallace 1978:448)

REFERENCES

Berkhafer, Robert F., Jr.
1972 Protestants, Pagans, and Sequences Among the North American Indians, 1760-1800. Pp. 370-381 in *The Emergent Native Americans: A Reader in Cultural Contact.* Deware E. Walker, ed. Boston: Little, Brown.

Callender, Charles
1978   Shawnee.   Pp. 622-635 in *Handbook of North American Indians,* vol. 15. Bruce G. Trigger, ed. Washington: Smithsonian Institution.

Deardorff, Merle H.
1951   The Religion of Handsome Lake: Its Origin and Development. Pp. 77-107 in Symposium on Local Diversity in Iroquois Culture. William N. Fenton, ed. *Bureau of American Ethnology Bulletin* 149. Washington.

Edmunds, R. David
1978 *The Pottowatomies; Keepers of the Fire.* Norman: University of Oklahoma Press.
1983   *The Shawnee Prophet.* Lincoln: University of Nebraska Press.

Forsyth, Thomas
1912 *Tribes of the Upper Mississippi Valley Region and the Region of the Great Lakes.* Emma H. Blair, ed. Cleveland: Arthur C. Clark Co.

Howard, James H.
1981 *Shawnee!: The Ceremonialism of a Native Indian Tribe and its Cultural Background.* Athens: Ohio University Press.

Hudson, John C.
1977 Theory and Methodology in Comparative Frontier Studies. Pp. 11-31 in *The Frontier: Comparative Studies,* vol. 1. David H. Milier and Jerome O. SteJFen, eds. Norman: University of Oklahoma Press.

Kendall, E. A.
1809 *Travels Through the Northern Parts of the United States in the Years 1807 and 1808.* New York.

Linton, Ralph
1943   Nativistic Movements. *American Anthropologist* 45:230-240.

Mooney, James
  1896 The Ghost Dance Religion and the Sioux Outbreak of 1890. Pp.
  653-1136 in *Fourteenth Annual Report of the Bureau of American
  Ethnology.* Washington.

  1910 Shawnee. Pp. 530-538 in Handbook of American Indians North
  of Mexico, vol. 2. Frederick W. Hodge, ed. Bureau *of American Ethnology Bulletin* 30. Washington.

  1910 Tecumseh. P. 714 in Handbook of American Indians North of
  Mexico, vol. 2. Frederick W. Hodge, ed. *Bureau of American Ethnology Bulletin* 30. Washington.

  1910   Tenskwatawa. Pp. 729-730 in Handbook of American Indians North of Mexico, vol. 2.   Frederick W. Hodge, ed.   *Bureau of
  American Ethnology Bulletin* 30. Washington.

Morrison, Alvin H., and David A. Ezzo
  1985 Dawnland Dualism in Northeastern Regional Context. Pp. 131-
  149 in *Papers Of The Sixteenth Algonquian Conference.* William
  Cowan, ed. Ottawa: Carleton University.

Overholt, Thomas W.
  1975 The Ghost Dance of 1890 and the Nature of the Prophetic
  Process. *Ethnohistory* 21:37-63.

Prince, Raymond
  1982   Shamans and Endorphins: Hypothesis for a Synthesis. *Ethos*
  10:409-423.

Raden, Paul
  1970   *The Winnebago Tribe.* Lincoln: University of Nebraska
  Press.

Schoolcraft, Henry R.
  1854   *Information Respecting the History, Condition and
  Prospects of the Indian Tribes of the United States,* vol. 4. Philadelphia: Lippincott, Grambo.

Tanner, John
  1830   *Narrative of the Captivity and Adventures of John Tanner
  During Thirty Years Among the Indians in the Interior of North America.* New York: G.C.H. Carvill.

Tooker, Elisabeth
   1978   The League of the Iroquois: Its History, Pohtics, and Ritual.
   Pp. 418-441 in *Handbook of North American Indians,* vol. 15. Bruce
   G. Trigger, ed. Washington: Smithsonian Institution.

Wallace, Anthony F.C.
   1978   *The Death and Rebirth of the Seneca.* New York: Knopf.

   1972 New Religions Among the Delaware Indians, 1600-1900. Pp.
   344-361 in *The Emergent Americans: A Reader in Cultural Change.*
   Deward E. Walker, ed. Boston: Little, Brown.

   1956   Revitalization Movements. *American Anthropoligist* 58:264-
   268

Chapter 3:

Female Status and the Life Cycle: A Cross-Cultural Perspective from Native North America

Introduction

The question of female status in egaliterian society is the central concern of this paper. Although female status varies in particular societies because of a variety of factors including universal cultural determinants (e.g., male strength and aggressiveness)) female reproduction and childbirth, children's socialization, economics and production relations and post-marital residence, this paper will explore the relationship between female status and the life cycle.

A variety of ethnohistorical evidence illustrates that in many Native societies females gained increased status with age. Brown (1982:143) has noted that "women's lives appear to improve with the onset of middle age. In some societies this change is dramatic and in others moderate."

A positive change in female status is clearly related to the onset of menopause which occurs during the social age-grade of middle age. Once a woman enters this stage, a variety of important changes take place in her social standing as the result of the biological phenomenon of menopause. Once a woman is past her childbearing years, the menstrual customs no longer apply to her, thus she receives freedom from male authority and also achieves a greater freedom of movement.

Older women exert authority over kinsmen and Brown (1982:144) has noted that "they have the right to extract labor from them or exercise decision making power over them." Older women also have a good deal of influence in the marriage arrangements in many societies.

Bart (1969) has pointed out that the "institutionalization of the mother-in-law and or grandmother role tends to be associated with higher status for middle-aged women."

There is ample evidence in the ethnohistorical and ethnographic literature that illustrates that "as women age beyond the childbearing years they are provided with new opportunities for achievement and for recognition beyond the household" (Brown 1982). The anthropological literature discusses a variety of roles for older women including: serving as mid wives (Hayes 1975; Paul and Paul 1975), holy women (Kolanda 1978; Hungry Wolf 1980), matchmakers (Wolf 1974), medicine women (Wright 1979a), curers (Spring 1976), and matrons (Brown 1970, 1982). All of these positions in which middle-aged women served provided them with increased status and public influence which went beyond the household.

I will now discuss a variety of roles for older females that are recorded in the ethnohistorical literature for several societies in Native North America including the Wabanaki, the Coastal Algonquians including the Delaware, Powhatan Confederacy tribes, Southern New England groups and the Iroquois.

The Wabanaki

Chamberlain provides several accounts that illustrate that females who had passed middle-age and entered the "grandame" rank had considerable status. Once a woman became a grandame she had a variety of privileges and duties that younger females did not have, including the ability to speak in councils and a much greater freedom from restraint (Chamberlain 1902:81, 85, 86; Morrison 1983:126, 127). Chamberlain also notes that older females were highly valued for their knowledge of herbs and roots used to cure the sick. The grandames also counseled both young and old in Wabanki society and Chamberlain notes that "The young people looked to her for guidance, the elders sought her counsel, and all dread her displeasure."

From Chamberlain's account it is clear the females in Wabankia had duties and privileges that were based on an age grading system. All females had some collective influence in the society but only older women, those who were grandames had individual influence in both religious and sociopolitical affairs.

The ethnohistorical record also supplies fragmentary evidence of Wabanki females who attained formal leadership positions. According to a Wabanki myth, Angel Queen was a female Wabanki sagamore or shaman who lived in the 16th century. A better account of formal female leadership in Wabanki society is provided by Christopher Levett. His account discusses the Queene of Quacke, who was a formal leader who obtained a leadership position by succession from her father (Levett 1983:104, 105).

Another female who inherited a formal position was Jacataqua of Swan Island, who inherited the role of sagamore from her mother. This stands in direct opposition to the stereotypical male-oriented hunting societies of the Dawnland (Griffiths 1976).

Eckstorm (1980) provides an account of a very important Penobscot Shaman named Molly Molasses. Molly Molasses was a very influential female Penobscot shaman in the 19th century. Thus older females or grandames among the Wabanki had a variety of roles in the society including serving as both political and relgious leaders. Older females in Wabankia clearly had individual influence in the public domain.

Coastal Algonquian Groups

Females in several Coastal Algonquian groups served as paramount sachems, spoke in councils, influenced war captains and marriages and functioned as shamans and traders.

John Smith mentioned the "Queene of Appamatuck" in his reports (1907:101). Smith said that the Queene was a "paramount sachem" of the Powhatan confedracy. He further recorded her presence in several confederacy councils, including the one that meditated his death (Grumet 1980:49). George Fox (1952:653) also noted the presence of female leaders in councils. He said "The Old Empress [of Accomack] ... sat in council" during his visit to their town in Maryland on March 24, 1673.

Robert Beverley (1947:232) mentioned that a female served as the political leader for the Pungoteque. He said the Pungoteque was governed by a Queen and although this was a small nation, of less than 20 families "she hath all the Nations of this shore under Tribute."

Female leadership was also present in the Esopus tribe, a Delawaran group that inhabited the western portion of the mid-Hudson valley in New York State. Grumet (1980:52) states that a group of both women and young men called "barebacks" forced the Esopus war captains to seek peace with the Dutch in 1664. Heckewelder (1876:161) noted that Delaware women had power over young men. He also reported that mothers had great influence in marriage arrangements and that they also served as marriage arbitrators. Women were also important as Shamans in the Coastal Algonquian groups. Simmons (1976:223) described a woman powwow in the Southern New England area. Elliot (1834:19), Gookin (1792:154) and Roger Williams (1866:149) also mention the importance and influence of female shamans. Tantaquidgeon (1972) and Heckewelder also stated that females served as shamans. Tantaquidegeon noted that females functioned as herbalists and love doctors whose supernatural power enabled them to communicate with the dead, to locate lost persons, and objects, and to fore-tell coming events. Heckewelder (1876:229) wrote that "there are physicians of both sexes who take considerable pains to acquire a correct knowledge of the properties and medical virtues of plants, roots, and barks."Elder shamans were believed to be especially powerful. Zeisberger noted that older male and female shamans had special medicine which gave them magical power (1910:83). He also stated that old women were often considered to be witches and were either feared, propitiated or burned. Snow (1976:283) also reported that female shamans were thought to be particularly powerful.

Females had an important function as traders in the Coastal Algonquian groups. Trading was a very important part of the economy in these societies and there are a number of reports in the ethnohistorical literature that discuss the importance of females as traders. An Englishmen who visisted the village of the Massachusetts Squaw sachem observed "almost all the women . . . sold their coats from their backs . . . [the English] promised them to come again to them, and they us to keep their skins" (Grumet 1980:56, 57). Heckewelder also remarked that females worked as traders (Heckewelder 1876:158).

John Juet (Henry Hudson's first mate), also mentioned that women served as traders: "there came eight and twentie Canoes full of men, women and children to betray us: but we saw their intent, and suffered none of them to come abord us ... They brought with them Oysters and Beanes, where we bought some" (Grumet 1980:57). A trader at Albany, New York stated that about 20% of his transactions "between 1695 and 1726 were made with women" (Norton 1974:28).

Thus all of this ethnohistorical evidence illustrates females served important political, economic and relgious functions in the Coastal Algonquian societies. It is clear that females gained status with increasing age and here again the relationship between status and age (life-cycle) is illustrated.

The Iroquois

The relationship between increased status and age is also very clear for the Iroquois matrons. The status and influence of the Iroquois females rested in the hands of the matrons or the elderly heads of households (Browr 1970). Randle (1951) has noted that any Iroquois female could aspire to become a matron. The Iroquois matrons had a variety of powers including influencing war parties, speaking in council, conferring titles and electing officials, removing officials, serving as ambassadors, and deter-mining issues of war and peace in times of crisis (Fenton 1986:36-38).

Marie de I'lncarnation stated that Iroquois matrons were "women of quality who had a deliberative voice in council, made decisions like men and it was they who delegated top ambassadors to treat peace" (Fentoi 1986:36).

Goldenweiser (1912:468) provided a brief statement that discusses the power of the Iroquoian matrons to elect and depose ruling elders: When a chief died, the women of his tribe and clan held a meeting at which a candidate for the vacant place was decided upon. A women delegate car-ried the news to the chiefs of the clans which belonged to the "side" of the deceased chief's clan. They had the power to veto the selection, in which case another women's meeting was called and another candidate selected.

The ethnohistorical record shows that Iroquois women had control over the land, agricultural tools and the means of production and distribu-tion of the goods. Women also controlled the distribution of surplus agri-cultural production. This surplus food was exchanged intertribally and therefore allowed the women to become more involved in political decision making (Parker 1912:234-236; Rothenberg 1981:69). Women also had sig-nificant influence on Iroquois war parties since they controlled the provi-sions that supplied these expeditions. The Iroquoian matrilocal residence pattern and the domestic arrangements of the longhouse reinforced a posi-tion of independence for Iroquois women (Ezzo 1988:54).

Conclusion

In conclusion the ethnohistorical record supplies ample evidence of a variety of role for females in Native North America. Females achieved positions of leadership in both religious and political spheres and in all of these societies females gained increased status once they reached middle-age. Thus clearly the life cycle is an important factor that must be consid-ered in any cross-cultural study of female status.

REFERENCES

Bart, Pauline
1969 Why Women's Status Changes in Middle Age: The Turns of the Social Ferris Wheel. *Sociological Symposium* 3:1-18.

Beverly, Robert
1947 *The History and Present State of Virginia.* Louis Wright, ed. Chapel Hill: The University of North Carolina Press. [1705.]

Brown, Judith K.
1970 Economic Organization and the Position of Women Among the Iroquois. *Ethnohistory* 17:151-167.
1982 Cross-Cultural Perspectives on Middle-Aged Women.   *Current Anthropology* 23:143-153.

Chamberlain, Montague
1902 The Primitive Life of the Wapanaki Women. *Acadiensis* 2: 75-86.

Eckstorm, Fannie Hardy
1980 *Old John Neptune and Other Maine Indian Shamans.* Orono, Maine: University of Maine Press. [1945.]

Eliot, John
1834 The Day-Breaking, if not the Sun-Rising of the Gospell with the Indians of New England. Pp. 1-23 in *Collections of the Massachusetts Historical Society,* 3rd series, Vol. 4. [1647.]

Ezzo, David A.
1988 Female Status in the Northeast. Pp. 49-62 in *Papers of the Nineteenth Algonquian Conference.* William Cowan, ed. Ottawa: C arleton University.

Fenton, William
1986   Leadership in the Northeastern Woodlands of North America. *American Indian Quarterly* Winter.21—44,

Fox, George
1952 *Journal of George Fox.* John L. Nickalls, ed. Cambridge: Cambridge University Press.

Goldenweiser, Alexander
1912 On Iroquois Work, 1912. Pp. 467-475 in *Summary Report of the Geological Survey of Canada, Anthropological Division, Sessional Paper* 26. Ottawa.

Gookin, Daniel
1792 Historical Collections of the Indians of New England. Pp, 141-229 in *Collections of the Massachusetts Historical Society,* 1st series, Vol. 1. [1624]

Griffiths, Linda
1976 Jactaqua. *Bates College Bulletin* 73:8.

Grumet, Robert Steven
1980 Sunskquas, Shamans, and Tradeswomen: Middle Atlantic Coastal Algonkian Women during the 17th and 18th Centuries. Pp. 43-62 in *Women and Colonization: Anthropological Perspectives.* Mona Etienne and Eleanor Leacock, eds. New York: Praegei.

Hayes, Rose Oldfield
1975 Female Genital Mutilation, Fertility Control, Women's Roles, and the Patrilineage in Modern Sudan: A Functional Analysis. *American Ethnologist* 2:617-633.

Heckeweldet, John
1876 History, Manners, and Customs of the Indian Nations. Memoirs *of the Pennsylvania Historical Society* 12. Philadelphia. [1818.]

Hungry Wolf, Beverly
1980 *The Ways of my Grandmothers.* New York; Morrow.

Kolanda, Pauline
1978 A Voyage into New England Begun in 1623 and Ended in 1624. Pp. 78-139 in *Christopher Levett of York, The Pioneer Colonist* in *Casco Bay.* James P. Baxter, ed. Portland, Maine: The Gorges Society. [1893.]

Morrison, Alvin H.
1983 Wabanki Women Extraordinaire: A Sampler From Fact and Fancy. Pp. 125-136 in *Papers of the Fourteenth Algonqvian Conference.* William Cowan, ed. Ottawa: Carleton University.

Norton, Thomas E.
1974 *The Fur Trade in Colonial New York, 1686-1776.* Madison: The University of Wisconsin Press.

Parker, Arthur C.
1912 Iroquois Uses of Maize and Other Food Plants. *New York State Museum Bulletin* 144. Albany: State University of New York.

Paul, Louis, and Benjamin Paul
1975 The Maya Midwife as a Sacred Specialist.   A Guatemalan Case.*American Ethnologist* 2:707-726.

Randle, Martha C.
1951 Iroquois Women Then and Now. Pp. 167-180 in *Bulletin of the Bureau of American Ethnology* 149. Washington.

Rothenberg, Diana B.
1980 The Mothers of the Nation. Pp. 63-87 in *Women and Colonization: Anthropological Perspectives*. Mona Etienne and Eleanor Leacock, eds. New York: Praeger.

Simmons, William S.
1976 Southern New England Shamanism: An Ethnographic Reconstruction. Pp. 217-256 in *Papers of the Seventh Algonquian Conference.* William Cowan, ed. Ottawa: Carleton University.

Smith, John
1907 *The General Historie of Virginia, New England and the Summer hies,* 2 vols. Glasgow: James Maclehose and Sons. [1624.]

Snow, Dean
1976 The Solon Petroglyphs and Eastern Abenaki Shamanism. Pp. 281-288 in *Papers of the Seventh Algonquian Conference.* William Cowan, ed. Ottawa: Carleton University.

Spring, Anita
1976 Epidemiology of Spirit Possession Among the Luvale of Zambia, Pp. 165-190 in Women in *Ritual and Symbolic Roles.* Judith Hoch-Smith and Anita Spring, eds. New York: Plenum.

Tantaquidgeon, Gladys
1972 Folk Medicine of the Delaware and Related Algonkian Indians. *Pennsylvania Historical and Museum Commission Anthropological Series* 3. Harrisburg.

Williams, Roger
1866 Key into the Language of America. *Publications of the Narragansett Club,* 1st series, Vol. 1. James H. Turnbull, ed. Providence.

Wolf, Margery
1974 Chinese Women: Old Skills in a New Context. Pp. 157-172 in *Women, Culture and Society.* M. Rosaldo and L. Lamphere, eds. Stanford: Stanford University Press

Zeisberger, David
1910 History of the North American Indians. Pp 1-109 in *Ohio Archaeological and Historical Publications,* Vol. 19. A.B. Hulber and W.N. Schwarze, eds. Cleveland.

Chapter 4:

Delaware Indian Land Claims: A Historical and Legal Perspective

In this paper we shall discuss Delaware Indian land claims in both a historical and legal context. The first section of the paper deals with the historical background necessary to understand the land claims filed by the Delaware. In the second part of the paper the focus is on a legal review of the Delaware land claims cases. Ezzo is responsible for the first section while Moskowitz is responsible for the second section.

1. History

The term Delaware has been used to describe the descendants of the Native Americans that resided in the Delaware River Valley and other adjacent areas at the start of the 17th century. The Delaware spoke two dialects: Munsee and Unami, both of these belong to the Eastern Algonquian Language family. Goddard has noted that the Delaware never formed a single political unit. He also has noted that the term Delaware was only applied to these groups after they had migrated from their original Northeastern homeland. Goddard sums up the Delaware migration as follows:

> The piecemeal western migration, in the face of white settlement and its attendant pressures during the eighteenth and nineteenth centuries, left the Delaware in a number of widely scattered places in Southern Ontario, Western New York, Wisconsin, Kansas and Oklahoma. Their history involves the repeated divisions and consolidations of many villages and of local, political and linguistic groups that developed in complicated and incompletely known ways. In addition, individuals, families and small groups were constantly moving from place to place. (Goddard 1978:213)

Tanner (1987:2) has correctly noted that the Delaware were the "most transient of all Indian people on the Great Lakes scene". To discuss all of the Delaware migrations would be beyond the scope of this paper (see Map 1). The purpose here is to outline the key Delaware subgroups and movements that are needed to properly understand the claims filed by the Delaware under the Indian Land Claims Commission.

Delaware Migrations Since Statehood

It is interesting to note, as Grumet (1989:90) has pointed out, that the Delaware maintained their traditional kinship system of three clans — Turtle, Turkey and Wolf, through all of their western migrations. Over time, however, these clans ceased to be matrilineal.

The Delaware raids on frontier settlements in Pennsylvania and Virginia ended in August 1794, when the Delaware were defeated at the Battle of Fallen Timbers on the Maumee River in Ohio. After the American Revolution, the demand by settlers for Ohio land cessions resulted in a number of treaties signed by the Delaware including the following: Fort Stanwix, 1784; Fort McIntosh, 1785; Fort Finey, 1786; and Fort Hamar, 1789 (Tanner 1987:69).

Tanner has noted that all of these treaties ceding Indian land were done at sparsely attended council meetings with inadequate Indian representation. At the treaty of Greenville in 1795 which followed Wayne's victory in 1794, two-thirds of the Ohio territory was ceded to the American Government. This land had been home to several Indian tribes including the Delaware, Shawnee, Mingo and Wyandot (see Map 2).

After the Greenville treaty, the main body of the Delaware left Ohio and accepted an invitation from the Piankasharo Indians and relocated to the White River in Indiana (Kraft 1986:236). Although the majority of the Delawares moved to Indiana, several subgroups did not. One group of Delaware moved to Missouri at the invitation of the Spanish Government in 1789. Another group, a Moravian mission band, established the town of Fairfield on the Thames River in Ontario in 1792. A third group of Munsee, settled among the Seneca in 1791 (Goddard 1978:223; see Map 3).

From 1790 to 1799 the American Congress passed four trade and intercourse acts relating to Indian Affairs and Commerce. Waldman (1985:190) has noted that this act "required federal approval and public treaty for the purchase of Indian land by states." In 1802 a new act was passed that codified the four previous ones. This act would become very important in Indian land claims filed under the Indian Land Claims Commission.

During the war of 1812, despite attempts by the British to persuade the Delaware to attack American settlements, they remained neutral. The Indian lands occupied by the main body of the Delaware along with the Mohicans and Munaees were originally obtained from the Miami and Pakashaw Indians in 1770 (Senate Report 1518:8, 1968). On December 12, 1808, President Thomas Jefferson signed a document which recognized this land transfer, stating that these three tribes and their descendants could remain on the White River "forever" (Senate Report 1518:8, 1968). In this case, forever for the Delaware would last only ten years.

Before discussing the westerly movements of the main body of the Delaware, the history of the group that would later be known as the Stockbridge-Munsee after this group had moved to Wisconsin in the 1830s should be outlined. After the American Revolution, in 1783, a group composed of both Munsee and Mahican moved to Canada (Brasser 1978:209). Another group of about 420 Mahicans accepted an invitation from the Oneida to relocate to a tract of land on Oneida Creek in New York. By 1786 most of the Indians had settled here at New Stockbridge.

Due to pressure from both White settlers and the Oneida, by 1791 Chief Sachem Hendrick Aupaumut was considering relocation. The Stockbridge removal was delayed, however, due to the efforts of Shawnee Chief Tecumseh who attempted to organize an anti-white Confederacy (Brasser 1978:209). In 1801, 63 Brotherton Indians (formerly of New Jersey) accepted an invitation to join the Mahican Indians at New Stockbridge (Kraft 1986:232).

Brasser has noted that in 1818, about seventy-five Stockbridges led by John Metoxen departed for Indiana. Upon their arrival, they learned that the Delaware and Miamis had been forced to sell their land. Missionaries then purchased some land from the Menominee and Winnebago Indians in Wisconsin for the Stockbridge (New York Indians). In 1828 a group of Indians from New Stockbridge settled on the Fox River in Wisconsin. They were led there by John W, Quinney. As of 1831, there were about 100 Delaware and 225 Stockbridges living on the Fox River.

The purchase of this land was disavowed by the Wisconsin Indians and the Stockbridge community was removed to Calumet County (east of Lake Winnebago) between 1832 and 1834. In 1837 a number of Moravian Munsee from Canada joined this group; thus they came to be called the Stockbridge-Munsee.

In 1837, John W. Quinney drafted a new tribal constitution that called for choosing tribal officers by election rather than by the traditional hereditary leadership system. This caused some dissension among the tribe which was increased by the efforts of the United States government to "extinguish

Indian claims east of the Mississippi." As a result, the Stockbridge agreed to cede half their land to the United States in return for money to finance removal. About 70 Stockbridge and about 100 Munsee left for the Missouri River in 1839. Many of these people did not survive the hardships of the move. Some joined the main body of Delaware in Kansas and a few went back to Wisconsin.

In 1856, the Stockbridge-Munsee were given a reservation in Shawano County, Wisconsin. About 150 Indians moved to this reservation in 1859. They were joined by a number of Brotherton and New York Iroquois. The Stockbridge-Munsee suffered a substantial loss of their land base due to the 1887 General Allotment Act.

In 1938, the Stockbridge-Munsee tribal constitution was approved by the Bureau of Indian Affairs under the Indian Reorganization Act of 1934. They were given 2,250 acres of land in Bartlane township. The current Stockbridge-Munsee population is about 1,000. In 1986, they filed a claim to six square miles of land that they formerly occupied in Madison and Oneida Counties in present-day New York State (see Map 7). A suit is still under review by the court and a judgment is expected soon in this case (Peg Rogers, personal communication).

The St. Mary's Treaty (1818)

The discussion will now return to the main body of the Delaware. The treaty of St. Mary's, Ohio, was signed on August 3, 1818. This treaty required the Delaware, Munsee, Mahicans and Nanticokes to give the United States occupancy rights to all their lands in Indiana (Newcomb 1956:97). The principal negotiators of the St. Mary's treaty were Chief William Anderson and Indian Agent John Johnstone (Senate Report 1518:9, 1968).

In return for their Indiana Lands the Delaware were promised land west of the Missouri on the James Fork of the White River (406 F. Supp. 1309, 1975:1318; Goddard 1978:229). The Delaware were given three years to relocate. A total of 1,346 Delaware and 1,499 horses completed the move (Kraft 1986:236).

The treaty of St. Mary's also illustrates the common United States government practice of only negotiating with a portion of the Indian tribal groups with rights to the land under review. In this case, for example, only some of the Stockbridge were present when the Indiana lands were ceded (406 F. Supp. 1309, 1975:1318).

The Stockbridge Mahican had written to Chief Anderson through Agent Johnstone advising him not to sell the Indian lands. Their message was never delivered. In a letter to Governor Cass on December 31, 1817, Agent Johnstone said, "I am doing everything in my power to prepare the minds of the Indians for a treaty. There is near 1,000 in New York in part civilized who will certainly immigrate to White River in a year or two and if they are once located there, it will be a difficult matter to purchase the country" (Senate Report 1518, 1968:9). B.F. Sticking, a United States Indian Agent to the Miami Indians also told Case in 1818: "The State of Indiana will push very hard at Washington to have something done [about White River lands] and to have it done in the spring, before the Mohegans can arrive from New York" (Senate Report 1518, 1968:9). Both of these Indian Agents were successful in their plans. The Indiana lands were ceded by treaty before a group of 60 Stockbridge-Mahican led by John Metaxen could arrive at the treaty grounds (Senate Report 1518, 1968:9).

The lands the Delaware received under this treaty were supposed to be of equal value to the ceded lands in Indiana. The tribe was also to receive a yearly sum of $4,000. Further, the United States agreed to pay the Delaware for improvements that they had made on their lands in Indiana. The Delaware filed a claim under the Indian Land Claims Commission for lack of proper compensation under this treaty (Smith 1947:451). This suit was successful, and the 1818 make-up of the tribe was used as one of the criteria of eligibility to share in the award money. Thus this included some of the Stockbridge who had migrated further west than the main body of the Delaware.

The Delaware in Missouri

The stay by the main body of the Delaware in Missouri was very short. In 1829, led by Chief Anderson, they signed another treaty with the United States. The Delaware ceded their Missouri lands as a part of this treaty. The Delaware had been under increasing pressure in Missouri from White settlers. For example, the discovery of a lead mine in Western Missouri resulted in the relocation of some Delaware (Kraft 1986:127). The Missouri land was poor in natural resources. The Delaware also suffered from hostilities with White settlers and with other tribes, especially the Osage and Pawnee. Conflicts with the Osage and Pawnee occurred over buffalo hunting territory. By this time, the Delaware had adopted the buffalo hunting subsistence pattern of "Plains" tribes. Kraft 91986:237) has noted that the Delaware "were accomplished horsemen, and their extended Buffalo hunts took them far to the south and west from their home."

The Delaware in Kansas

The main body of the Delaware moved to a new reservation north of the Kansas River in 1831. The Kansas reservation is what the Delaware received in the 1829 treaty. This was a part of the payment that the Delawares were owed by the United States in exchange for their lands ceded in 1818. However, it must be noted that there was a large disparity in value between the Indiana lands and the Kansas lands. This was to form the basis for a claim brought before the Indian Land Claims Commission (Docket #337) which shall be discussed later in this paper

Other Delaware Migrations After The 1829 Treaty

Although the main body of the Delaware did relocate to Kansas in 1831, several subgroups did not. One portion of the Delaware remained in sections of Oklahoma and Texas. The Texas Delawares were placed on a reservation on the Brazos River in 1854. Due to pressure from local settlers this group was relocated to the Washita River in Indian Territory (Oklahoma) in 1859; they then merged with the Delaware already living in Oklahoma (Goddard 1978:224; see Map 3).

Another group of Delaware who were en route from Texas to Kansas obtained permission from the Choctaw in 1853 to stay on its land as tenants in Anadarko, Oklahoma (see Map 3). Although some of this group did eventually move to Kansas, most of them remained in Oklahoma. The descendants of this group now reside among the Wichita and Caddo Indians at Anadarko, Oklahoma. This group is now known as the Absentee Delaware of Western Oklahoma (406 F. Supp. 1309, 1975.1318).

Tanner (1987:123) has noted that in 1830, "about 200 Shawnee and Delaware along with their long-term Cherokee Allies, had found refuge in Caddo Country south of the Red River on the Texas borderland, All of these tribes had long engaged in joint warfare against the Osage." Tanner has also noted that by 1830, about 300 Stockbridge-Munsee had moved to Wisconsin.

The Munsee group of the Delaware were the most dispersed of all. This group broke down into several subgroups. After the American Revolution, many of the Munsee migrated to Ontario to live on the Grand River or the Thames River with some of the Iroquois who had been led there by Joseph Brant (see Map 3). Most of the Munsee remained in Ontario but one group did move in 1837 from Moraviantown and Munceytown to Kansas. Still another Munsee group that did not join up with the main body of the Delaware in Kansas moved in with the Chippewas, with whom their descendants remain today. The Canadian Munsee group that did relocate to the Kansas reservation included descendants from other former Eastern tribes including the Mohicans, Nanticokes and Connoys.

Treaty Sale of the Kansas Lands

On May 6, 1854, the main body of the Delaware ceded part of their Kansas residence lands and the hunting outlet lands (see Map 5). The ceded residence lands were to be sold at public auction with the proceeds from the sale going into the Delaware tribal fund (406:1310). However, in 1856 and 1857, the United States Government did not sell the lands by public auction as required by the 1854 treaty. Thus the Delaware "received far less than they should have realized from the sale of their lands" (406 F. Supp. 1309, 1975:1319). This act by the government would become the basis for the Indian Land Claims Commission judgment in Dockets 72 and 298 (406 F. Supp. 1309, 1975:1319).

In an 1860 treaty (12 Stat. 1129) the United States surveyed the diminished Delaware reserve in order to allot each Delaware an 80-acre tract (Treaty Article 1). Article Iv of this treaty set aside 80-acre tracts for Absentee Delaware who were expected to rejoin the main body of Delaware in Kansas (406 F. Supp. 1309, 1975:1319).

In 1866 the Delaware ceded the remainder of their Kansas land for territory in Oklahoma on unoccupied Cherokee lands. Each of the Delaware was to receive 160 acres of land in Oklahoma. At this time the adult Delaware were given the option of remaining in Kansas. Those that took this option had to dissolve their relationship with the tribe. They would become United States citizens. Each of them would be given an 80-acre tract of land and would receive their allotment of money from the tribal fund. The key point is that, after this, these individuals could not share in any future Delaware property or annuities. A total of 21 adults and 49 minors took this option and appear on the Kansas Delaware registry (406 F. Supp. 1309, 1975:1319). Minors were considered temporarily severed from the tribe until age 21. Upon reaching 21 they would elect to become United States citizens or could relocate to the Cherokee Delaware in Oklahoma (406 F. Supp. 1309, 1975:1320). This historical action would also become the basis for a Delaware claim filed under the Indian Land Claims Commission.

All of the Delaware who relocated to Oklahoma received 160 acres of land in the Cherokee Nation (Kraft 1986:238). A total of 985 Delaware thus became part of the Cherokee tribe. They paid $1.00 per acre for a tract of land along the Little Verdigris (or Canes) River, in Northeastern Oklahoma in present Washington County (Kraft 1986:238).

Delaware and Cherokee Relations

The Delaware discovered that the Cherokee were not especially friendly toward them. One source of conflict between the two tribes was due to the sides taken by each during the Civil War. The vast majority of the Delaware, a total of 170, fought for the Union while the majority of the Cherokee had fought on the Confederate side (Grumet 1989:85). The terms pressed on the Delaware by the Cherokee were as follows:

1. The Delaware had to become Cherokee citizens.
2. The Delaware would be governed by the Cherokee.
3. The Cherokee demanded that the registered Delaware share with them their tribal funds.   They in turn, however, refused to share the Cherokee tribal funds with the Delaware (Grumet 1989:86).   This term would become the basis for a suit filed by the Delaware against the Cherokee.

Background Information to the Delaware-Cherokee Law Suit

The agreement that the Delaware signed with the Cherokee in 1867 resulted in the termination of the Delaware tribe as a political unit. The Delaware become Cherokee citizens and purchased 157,000 acres of land for which they paid a total of $157,000. The Delaware also paid $121,824.28 for Cherokee citizenship rights. The Delaware were told by both the United States and the Cherokee government that "they would have equal rights, along with native-born Cherokee citizens, to all the remaining lands and funds owned by the Cherokee Nation" (Weslager 1972:451).

In response to a formal request from principal Cherokee chief, J.B. Mayes, the United States government decided to distribute to the Delaware all of the remaining funds from their tribal account. The first installment of $425,000 was paid out to 836 Delaware in December of 1891. This amounted to $508 per person. A second payment was made in August of 1893 of $459,644 or $527.72 per person. These funds were supposed to be used for home improvements by the Delaware.

About this same time, the Delaware and Cherokee became involved in controversies over fiscal matters. The Cherokee received money from the United States for land sales to pioneer families and from cattle ranch leases. All receipts from these sales were given out to Cherokee citizens on a per capita basis. Weslager (1972:446) has noted that "in May of 1883, the

Cherokee National Council denied the Delaware the right to participate with the other Cherokee citizens in the distribution of funds received from the sale of grasslands of the Arkansas River."

The Delaware took the position that they were entitled to share in these funds by virtue of the treaty of 1866. They insisted that is was the obligation of the United States government to protect and support their position on this issue. If the government would not support their position they wanted to recieve the $279,424.28 they had paid for the land and Cherokee citizenship rights refunded to them plus their $900,000 former Delaware national account which had been spent to improve lands in the Cherokee nation. Further they requested new land were they could settle and resume their former tribal organization (Weslager 1972:447).

Charles Journeycake, a modernist Delaware who functioned as a Baptist preacher, was selected by a group of six other modernists to represent the tribe in court proceedings. Journeycake was contracted for the recovery of a number of items including:

1. Money due the Delaware from the Cherokee Nation.
2. Money from lands given up in Kansas which were not paid for.
3. Cash for timber illegally taken from lands in Kansas which was not paid for.
4. Compensation for ponies and cattle stolen from the tribe while in Kansas. (Weslager 1972:447)

The United States Court of Claims issued a judgment supporting the Delaware position (Smith 1947:459). The Cherokee appealed this decision and it then went to the Supreme Court. The Supreme Court upheld the lower court's ruling by noting that the Delaware were, due to the 1867 agreement, citizens of the Cherokee Nation "and as such, entitled to equal rights with all the other Cherokee citizens in proceeds from the sale of lands or any other income disbursed to Cherokee citizens" (Weslager 1972:449).

Shortly after this decision, another series of problems arose between the Delaware and Cherokee. This time the issue concerned oil, gas and coal resources that were found on land occupied by the Delaware. Some of the Cherokee businessmen obtained mineral leases which were then subleased to prospectors and business organizations. These individuals in turn sank oil wells on Delaware land and claimed that these mineral leases gave them preferred right to the mineral resources of the land to the total exclusion of the Delaware residents (Weslager 1972:450).

There was corruption and bribery taking place among the Cherokee officials and a faction unfriendly to the Delawares had gained control of both branches of the Cherokee National Council. The Cherokee government then took the position that the Delawares did not have any ownership rights to the lands they were living on and had paid for. This dispute ended up as a claim filed before the Indian Land Claims Commission.

The General Allotment or Dawes Act

The General Allotment or Dawes Act was passed in 1887. The Cherokee Nation accepted allotment in 1902. This dissolved the Cherokee Nation and abolished the reservation and thus forced acceptance of United States citizenship on all former members of the Cherokee Nation, including the Delaware (Grumet 1989:93). The central goal of the General Allotment Act was to allow the Native Americans to own private plots of land. This act, which became law in 1887, was one of the most devastating implements of United States assimilation policies ever devised. This act required that all tribally held reservation lands be divided into separately owned plots. Heads of households were usually given 160 acres. One of the major problems with this act was that government Indian agents were allowed to determine who was considered a household head. Most Indian Agents totally ignored traditional clan affiliations or family groupings in determining this (Grumet 1989:91). This law severely weakened tribal ties along with terminating communal property. The law also provided more land to homesteaders. Parcels remaining were considered surplus land and sold off to non-Indians.

Waldman (1985:178) has noted that as a result of the Dawes and Curtis Act (1898), which dealt with inheritance laws, "the Indian land base shrunk from about 150 million acres to about 60 million acres". He also notes that as early as 1889 "two million acres of land had been bought from the Indians, usually at ridiculously low prices, and thrown open to white settlement in the land run" (Waldman 1985:183; see land ad, illustration 6).

The results of the Dawes Act for the Delaware were as follows. First, the Cherokee Nation was dissolved and all Delaware became United States citizens. Second, each of the 890 registered Delaware were allotted an average of 60 acres of land. Many of these land allotments were a considerable distance from established Delaware communities. Third, the remainder of the 157,000 acres of land claimed by the Delaware was sold off to non-Indians.

The Delaware in the 20th Century

On April 1904, Congress awarded $150,000 to resolve all outstanding claims of the Delaware living in the former Cherokee Nation. The Delaware were represented by Richard C. Adams, a Delaware Christian preacher (Grumet 1989:99). Congress refused to restore Delaware tribal status and thus lost lands could not be recovered by the tribe. The allotment of tribal land to individual Delaware and the sale of the "surplus" land was completed by 1910. In the 1920s an oil boom swept Oklahoma. Oil was found on some of the Delaware lands but tribal loss of mineral rights kept the Delaware from benefiting from its discovery. In 1924 the United States granted citizenship status to all Native Americans. In 1934 the IRA Act was passed by the Roosevelt Administration. This act was intended to protect existing tribal governments. The act set forth a procedure to recognize tribes who voted to adopt a constitution providing for a representative form of government. The Stockbridge-Munsee were the only American Delawares to earn IRA recognition (Grumet 1989:99). The Stockbridge-Munsee were given recognition on May 21, 1938. As a result of this they were able to purchase a 15,000-acre reservation in Wisconsin with funds received from the federal government.

Current Status of the Delaware

Approximately 13,000 people are on the Delaware tribal rolls recognized by the United States and Canada. Federally recognized tribal governments operate on the Canadian Delaware Reserve and on the Stockbridge-Munsee reservation in Wisconsin. The Stockbridge-Munsee population is about 1,000.

The General Claims Process

The Federal Court of Claims was created in 1855. Access to this court was not granted to a tribe until 1881. In 42 years only 38 cases reached the court and only 17 resulted in awards to Indians (Hagan 1988:19).

In 1946, Congress signed into law the Indian Claims Commission Act. This was done as a part of the eventual goal of termination for all United States Indian Tribes. President Truman noted that the United States purchased more than 90 percent of the territory of the country from the Native Americans at a price of 800 million dollars. The President said that it would be a miracle "if in the course of these dealings ... we had not made some mistakes and occasionally failed to live up to the precise terms of our treaties and agreements with some 200 tribes. But we stand ready to submit all such controversies to the judgment of impartial critics. We stand ready to correct any mistakes we have made" (quoted from Hagan 1988:21).

There are three key basic points that must be noted in reference to the Indian Land Claims Commission. First, claims made in reference to individual Indians could not be reviewed. Second, Indians who lost land when reservations were broken up, could not be reimbursed under the Indian Claims Commission. Third, decisions of the Commission would only involve financial compensation. No land would be returned to the tribe making a claim (Hagan 1988:21).

The Indian Land Claims Cases: The Process

Hagan (1988:21-23) has pointed out some key items to note in reference to the Indian Land Claims Cases. In all of these cases testimony was heard to establish the claims of the Indians in reference to the land area in question. The fair market value of the land was estimated as of the time of the land cession. This amount was then compared to the actual amount paid minus any government offsets. Expert testimony was presented in these cases by both anthropologists and historians. The Indian Land Claims commission did not consider the land's potential value with regard to mineral rights. Another problem in these cases involved the use of the term "unconscionable consideration". This term was used to describe the degree of underpayment for Indian lands but it was never precisely defined or universally applied. All awards made by the ICC had to be appropriated by Congress. The distribution of the award was often a very complex and lengthy process. Only tribes with claims made against the United States could file under the ICC act. Claims made to address compensation under state actions were not covered by this act. The 1790 Trade and Intercourse Act has been used by lawyers representing Indians with claims filed to challenge the improper actions of states that were not authorized under the Trade and Intercourse Act to conduct treaty signings with the Indians.

2. Delaware Case Reviews

Prior to dealing with the case law a review of several American Indian Law concepts is required. Legal systems are designed to bring structure and organization to society. This in turn allows governments to Function and interact with the population. Legal systems provide a means to direct, protect and affect groups within society. To do this legal systems often must create legal fictions to allow government action. This is very apparent in the area of Indian Law in the United States. The legal concepts of "aboriginal title" and the "discovery doctrine" are two important examples.

The concept of "aboriginal title" has a history going back to feudal land laws and seventeth century Spanish theology (Vescey and Starna 1988:37). In American Indian Law it was first spelled out by Chief Justice John Marshall in *Johnson v. McIntosk,* 21 U.S.(*Wheat.) 543(1823). The court saw the Indians as having title to the land based on their exclusive and actual use of it "from time immemorial". This did not give them the legal ability to dispose of the land since the "discovery doctrine" had given overall control to the federal government. This doctrine also pre-dates the federal government. It was the legal basis for European colonization and purchase of lands inhabited by Native Americans. The doctrine basically held that the land has been "discovered by the sovereign", the King of England for example. This "discovery" gave the sovereign full title to all aboriginal lands. It then recognized the right of the Indians to continue to occupy and use the land they were on. The doctrine held that only the sovereign or his representative could end the Indian rights of occupancy. This legal theory further held that the Indians could not sell their land to anyone other than the sovereign. The United States adopted this doctrine, claiming it had gained absolute title over the land from the English Crown and other European sovereigns via treaties and conquests.

The U.S. Supreme Court in the *McIntosh* case held that:

> They were admitted to be the rightful occupants of the soil [the Indians], with a legal as well as just claim to retain possession of it, and to use it according to their own discretion: but their rights to complete sovereignty, as independent nations, were necessarily diminished, and their power to dispose of the soil at their own will, to whomsoever they pleased, was denied by the original fundamental principle, that discovery gave exclusive title to those who made it [the Americans and Europeans]. 21 U.S. (*Wheat.) at 574

By this holding only the United States government could extinguish occupancy rights of federally recognized Indian tribes and groups.

The modern version of this concept is explained in the case of *Oneida Indian Nation v. County of Oneida,* 414 U.S. 661(1974). This case held that although Indians had aboriginal title or original title, the federal government only could end such title. This could be done through purchase or seizure.

In order for a tribe to claim damages against the government it often must prove it had "recognized title" to the land or resources in question. This means that at the time in question, the tribe had federally recognized title by treaty or law to the land. A violation of such title by the government is a "taking" under the Fifth Amendment and subject to compensation *(Untied States v. Creek Nation,* 295 U.S. 103(1935)).

There are two other items of importance that should at least be mentioned before moving on. One is the 1790 *Non-Intercourse Act* and the second is the Indian Claims Commission. The *Non-Intercourse Act,* which is still good law, prohibits states from making any treaty or transaction with a federally recognized Indian tribe after 1790. This law was the basis for several modern suits by tribes in the eastern United States. It is the basis for a current ongoing suit by the Stockbridge-Munsee against the State of New York (Rogers 1992). The Indian Claims Commission was established in 1946 to be the forum for claims and suits against the United States. Until Congress disbanded the Commission in 1978, the ICC heard hundreds of cases. Appeal to higher federal courts was allowed. The records of the ICC are filled with an amazing amount of historic detail. This is also true of the federal court records involving those cases that were appealed from the Claims Commission. Those that are interested should review Canby's *American Indian Law in a Nutshell* (1988) which provides a clear and brief summary of this legal field.

The Delaware Cases

Cherokee Nation v. Journeycake, 155 U.S. 196(1894): In the 1880s a disagreement between the Cherokee Council and the Delaware developed over the question of proceeds from land sales on the Cherokee Reservation. The Cherokee felt the Delaware were not entitled to the money. The Delaware brought suit in the U.S. Court of Claims. The suit claimed that the 1866 treaty and 1867 agreement with the Cherokee made the Delaware full citizens of the Cherokee Nation, entitled to share in the tribe's funds and property. The Delaware said that if the government did not support their position, they would request a return of all money paid by them (the Delaware) to the Cherokee for land. In addition the Delaware would seek return of the $900,000 tribal fund that had been used to improve the lots of land purchased from the Cherokee. Also, the Delaware would demand new lots of land to rebuilt on. Probably to head off a disaster, the Court of Claims upheld the Delaware claims to the sale money as provided in the treaties. The Cherokee appealed to the United States Supreme Court, which held in an 1894 decision that indeed the treaty of 1866 and the 1867agreement made the Delaware who had relocated to the Cherokee

Reservation citizens of that tribe. The court held that these Delaware were, in fact entitled to share in the property and funds of the Cherokee Nation.

Delaware Indians v. Cherokee Nation, 193 U.S. 127(1904): This case grew out of the first suit described above. It dealt with the issue of land ownership and fair compensation. A suit was filed in Claims Court to determine the property rights of the Delaware on Cherokee land. In addition the money owed to the Delaware as a result of the *Journeycake* decision still had not been paid. The court was asked to rule on this matter as well. The United States Court of Claims held that the Delaware did not have perpetual title to the lands set aside for them on the Cherokee reserve in 1867. The court further held that they had only purchased the right of life occupancy, with additional rights dependent on the allotment process. The Delaware appealed and in 1904, the United States Supreme Court upheld the decision of the lower court. The Supreme Court cited the fact that under U.S. law the Cherokee did not have title to their lands, so they could not have conveyed a fee simple title (right of absolute ownership) to the Delaware. The court ruled that it was the United States government that held the land in trust for the tribes.

United States v. Delaware Tribe of Indians, 427 F. 2d 1218(1970): This case was an appeal by the United States and a cross appeal by the tribe from a decision of the Indian Claims Commission. The ICC had allowed an offset of any award to an Indian tribe whose gratuities amounting to more than 5% of a principal sum paid to the tribe. The U.S. Court of Claims had affirmed in part and reversed in part the ICC ruling on a Delaware suit on the amount of money paid for their old Kansas lands. The ICC had denied the Delaware claims that they had been underpaid for the outlet strip of land in Kansas. The Court of Claims reversed that decision. After a rehearing the Court of Claims determined that the land had been worth $617,980, but the tribe had only been paid $10,000 at the time. The claims court held that the Delaware were entitled to the difference. There was no provision to convert 1867 prices to 1970 prices in making the award.

The only question remaining was what offsets, if any, should be deducted from the judgment. The tribe also took issue with the ICC on the size of the land in question. The tribe felt that the Kansas strip contained more than the 960,000 acres allowed for by the ICC.

The United States government appealed the ICC's ruling to allow the gratuitous offsets of money already paid and not to allow any credit to the government for lands the government claimed to have given the Delaware on the Wichita Reserve. The Delaware appealed the ICC's ruling that the lands in question were only 960,000 acres and that the government was allowed to credit $150,000 paid to the tribe in earlier suits.   The Federal

District Court reviewed this appeal and upheld the ICC, except the court overturned the ICC on the issue of offsets. The court said $72,600.37 could be offset from the amount owed to the tribe under the 5% rule used by the ICC.

Weeks v. United States, 406 F. Supp. (W.D. Okla. 1975): This case was the product of the Absentee-Delaware and the Cherokee-Delaware legal victory in several Indian Claims Commission rulings against the United States. These suits had been initiated in the 1950s and 1960s. They were claims for violations of the Treaty of 1818 and the Treaty of 1854. One of the major violations was the selling of Delaware lands at private auction at below market price, thus depriving the tribe of large amounts of money. The Delaware had prevailed in these claims after many years of litigation. In the late 1960s Congress enacted legislation to award the Delaware the money. A determination of who was eligible to collect this award money then had to be made (25 U.S.C.S., 1967:1141-1147; 25 U.S.C.S., 1968:1181-1186; P.L. 90-508: 82 Stat. 861, 1968).

In the original guidelines the eligibility rules were somewhat broad. As a result over 1500 petitions from Munsee Indians were received by the Bureau of Indian Affairs. This delayed the settlement, since each one had to be reviewed and all appeals had to be heard. The Delaware Business Committee, which had lead the drive to make the claims on behalf of the two Oklahoma Delaware groups, brought pressure on the government to only allow a restricted group to share in the cash settlement. They proposed that only those people born on or prior to the settlement date, who could trace their lineal ancestry to the 1906 Delaware Indian per capita payroll, or to the base census role of the Absentee Delaware Tribe of Western Oklahoma made in 1940; or could prove their lineal ancestry back to the main body of the tribe as it was constituted at the 1818 Treaty of St. Mary's. In addition to all of the above, claimants had to be current U.S. citizens to qualify to receive award money.

Even though many of the Munsee ancestors had been historically part of the Delaware people, the Oklahoma groups contended that they had broken away from the Delaware and had become separate tribes. This, of course, was true to some degree. The U.S. government adopted these requirements which prevented those Munsee or Delaware descendants living in Canada or as part of the Stockbridge-Munsee and Brotherton Indians from taking part in the settlement.

The two Delaware groups in Oklahoma (Absentee and Cherokee) thought the way was now clear to receive the money awarded them by the court. This changed when the Kansas-Delaware filed suit in federal court, claiming that they, too, were entitled to share in the money. The Kansas group argued that their ancestors were a part of the main body of the Delaware tribe at the time of both the 1818 and 1854 treaties when the harm had been done. The lower federal court upheld the claims of the Kansas-Delaware, finding that to exclude them from the award violated the "equal protection" clause of the U.S. Constitution. The court said that the ancestors of this group were indeed part of the tribe at the times in question, and as such met the criteria to receive award money. The two Oklahoma Delaware groups and the U.S. government appealed. The case went up to the U.S. Supreme Court, the description of which follows.

Delaware Tribal Business Committee v. Weeks, 430 U.S. 73(1977): The U.S. Supreme Court in an eight-to-one decision reversed the lower federal court ruling. The court held that even though the ancestors of the Kansas Delaware had been part of the main tribe at the time of both the 1818 and 1854 treaties they had ended their relationship with the Delaware tribe by their actions under the 1866 treaty. The ancestors of the Kansas Delaware had taken an option under the 1866 treaty which allowed them to stay on their land in Kansas while the bulk of the tribe was removed to Oklahoma. The treaty option allowed those Delaware who wished to stay in Kansas to do so. They would receive U.S. citizenship, a plot of land and some money. In exchange they had to renounce their ties to the Delaware Nation and could not claim any right to tribal funds or property. The court held that this was a valid treaty and that Congress had acted within its authority. This meant that the descendants of the Kansas Delaware who had brought the suit could claim no part of any award given to the Delaware Indians. Legally they could not claim Delaware Indian status, despite the fact that they were in reality of Delaware stock.

This decision finally freed the award money. It could now be dispersed to those who qualified under the guidelines mentioned earlier. In July of 1977, a cheque free from any taxes, for $1,399.59 was sent to each of the 9,608 approved claimants (Wealager 1978:247). In addition 10% of the award money was palced into a tribal fund (25 U.S.C.S., 1967:1141-1147).

Stockbridge-Munsee Litigation

It is interesting to note that the Stockbridge-Munsee of Wisconsin are currently involved in a suit against the State of New York. I include this because many of the Stockbridge-Munsee can trace their lineage back to the Munsee elements of the Delaware. The suit involves the land in upstate New York that the Stockbridge-Munsee lived on in the early 1800s (see Map 7).

New York purchased it when the tribe moved on to Wisconsin. Since this took place after the 1790 *Non-Intercourse Act,* the tribe began a suit in the early 1980s claiming the land sale was in violation of the Act and New York owed the tribe compensation.   In light of the several successful suits by tribes on these grounds against eastern states, the tribe felt it had a fair chance at winning this case. Litigation has gone on now for several years. The case took a new turn in late 1991. The state raised an Eleventh Amendment defense. The Eleventh Amendment to the U.S. Constitution protects states from a variety of types of suits in federal court, particularly suits for money by private citizens. There are exceptions to this and both sides have submitted extensive briefs to the court. As of this writing, the court has yet to rule on the case (Rogers 1992).

Conclusion

We have attempted to provide a brief outline of the attempts by the Delaware to seek redress in U.S. courts. It is by no means a full account. The records of the ICC cases involving the Delaware alone could make a very long book. These cases are an interesting place to start in reviewing Delaware history as they were forced westward. An understanding of the history of the Delaware and a knowledge of their major western movements is essential in order to attempt to understand the context of the Delaware land claim cases. Both the Delaware historical movements and the land claim cases illustrate the struggle they have faced in trying to preserve their own culture within the context of the larger non-Indian society.

Acknowledgments

1. To Chelsea House publishers and artist Gary Tong for use of three maps that appeared in Robert Grumet's book on the Lenapes (1989).
2. To Harry DeBan for drawing two maps. The map of Indian territory was based on a map that appeared in Waldman (1985:181). The Stockbridge-Munsee claim area map was based on a map that appeared in Vessey and Starna (1988:4).
3. To the library of Congress for granting permission to use the land add. The land add shown in this paper was an enlarged version of one that appeared in Grumet (1989:92).
4. To Bob Fly for his computerized version of the Delaware historic period migration map. This map was based on one that appeared in Kraft (1986:234).
5. To Dr. Ives Goddard for reading an earlier version of this paper. His comments helped to clarify a point on the Stockbridge Mahican.
6. To William T. Hagan for providing several suggestions on references.
7. To Peg Rogers for providing Michael Moskowitz with a telephone update of the current Stockbridge-Munsee law suit,
8. To Ronald P. Koch for proofreading the paper.

REFERENCES

Brasser, T.J.
    1978 Mahican. Pp.   198-212 in   *Handbook of North American Indians* Vol. 15: *Northeast.* Bruce G. Trigger, ed. Washington: SmithsonianInstitution.

Bureau of Indian Affairs
    1984 *Report of Stockbridge-Munsee.* Washington, D.C.: Office of Public Affairs, BIA.

Goddard, Ives
    1978 Delaware.   Pp. 213-239 in *Handbook of North* American *Indians,* Vol.   15: *Northeast.* Bruce G. Trigger, ed. Washington: Smithsonian Institution.

Grumet, Robert S.
    1989 *The Lenapes.* New York, Chelsea House.

Hagan, William T.
    1988 To Correct Certain Evils. Pp. 17-31 in *Iroquois Land Claims.* Christopher Vecsey and William A. Starna, eds. Syracuse: Syracuse University Press.

Kraft, Herbert C.
    1986 *The Lenape: Archaeology, History and Ethnography.* Newark: New Jersey Historical Society.

Newcomb, William W.
    1956 The Culture and Acculturation of the Delaware Indians.   *University of Michigan Museum of Anthropology, Anthropological Papers* 10. Ann Arbor.

Rogers, Peg
    1992 Telephone Interview. 3 Feburary 1992.

Tanner, Helen Hornbeck
    1987 *Atlas of Great Lakes Indian History.* Norman: University of Oklahoma Press.

Waldman, Carl
    1985 *Atlas of the North American Indians.* New York: Facts of File Publications.

Weslager, C.A.
    1972 *The Delaware Indians: A History.* New Brunswick, N.J.: Rutgers

University Press.
    1978 *The Delaware Indian Westward Migration.* Wallinford, Pennsylvania: Middle Atlantic Press.

LEGAL SOURCES

Canby, William C, Jr.
1988 *American Indian Law in a Nutshell.* 2nd ed. St. Paul,
Minnesota: West Publishing Company.
Delaware Tribal Business Committee v. Weeks, 430 U.S. 73 (1977).
Delaware Indians v. Cherokee Nation, 193 U.S. 127 (1904).
Cherokee Nation v, Journeycake, 155 U.S. 196 (1894).
Weeks v. United States, 406 F. Supp. 1309 (W.D. Okla. 1975).
Emigrant New York Indians. Distribution of Judgment Fund, 25 U.S.C.S.,
114— 1147 (Law. Coop. 1967).
Delaware Nation of Indians, 25 U.S.C.S., 1181-1186 (Law. Co-op. 1968).
Indians-Delaware Nation-Disposition of Funds, P.L. 90-508; 82 Stat.
861. Senate Report 1518, 90th Cong, 2d sess. (1968).

Smith E.B.
1947 *Indian Tribal Claims. 2* vols. Washington, D.C: University
Publications of America.
Johnson v, McIntosh, 21 U.S. (Wheat) 543 (1823).
Oneida Indian Nation v. County of Oneida, 414 U.S. 661 (1974).
United States v. Creek Nation, 295 U.S. 103 (1935).

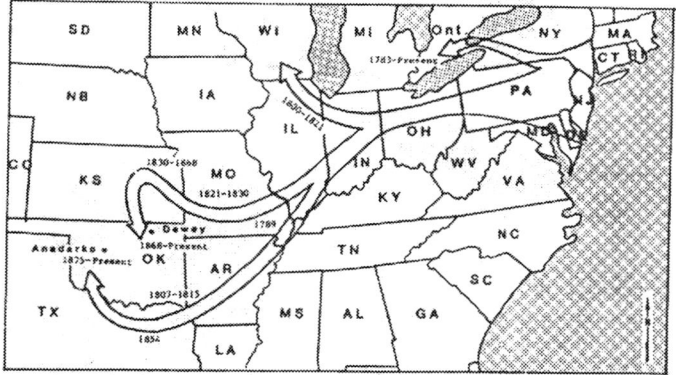

Fig. 40. Map showing the migration routes of the Delaware and Munsee Indians following the signing of the Treaty of Easton in 1758. Many
Munsee settled in Ontario, Canada, and in Wisconsin and Kansas. Large
numbers of Lenape finally settled in Oklahoma, following stops in Pennsylvania, Ohio, Indiana, Missouri, and Kansas. The dates are indicated
on the map. The "Absentee Delaware," now the Delaware Tribe of Western Oklahoma, veered southwestward; from settlements in Arkansas and
Texas, they finally relocated near Anadarko, Oklahoma. Modified after a
map in C. A. Weslager, *The Delaware Indian Westward Migration* (Wall-
ingford, Pa.: The Middle Atlantic Press, 1978).

Map 1:   From Robert Fly, based on Kraft 1986:234.

Map 2: From Chelsea House Publishers and Gary Tong (artist); from Grumet 1989.

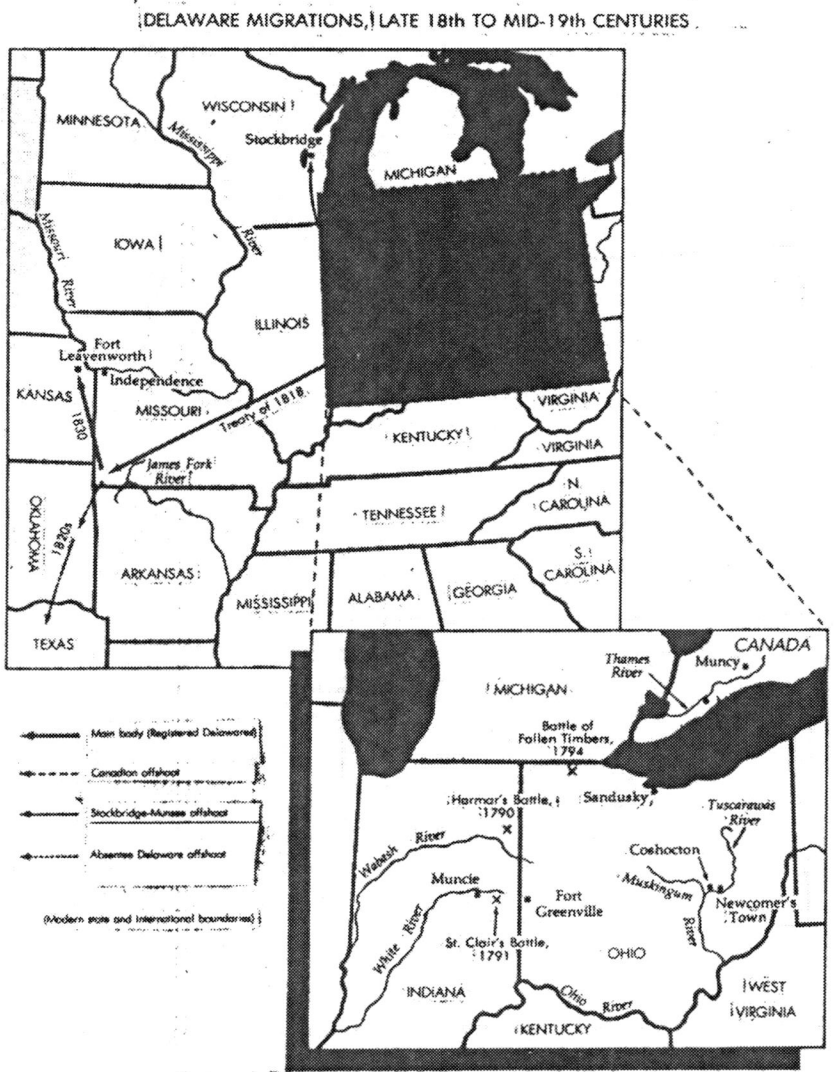

Map 3:   From Chelsea House Publishers and Gary Tong (artist);
from Grumet 1989.

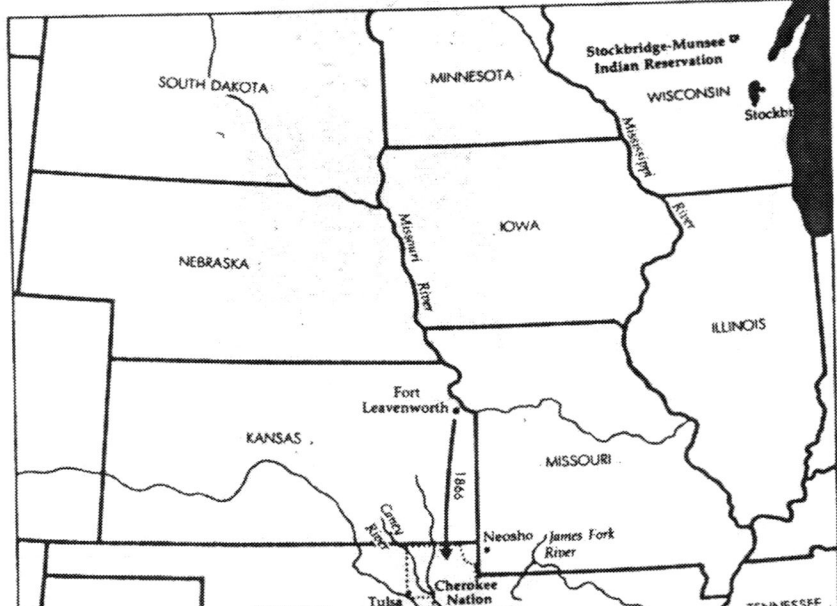

THE DELAWARES AND STOCKBRIDGE-MUNSEES, LATE 19th AND EARLY 20TH CENTURIES

Map 4:   From Chelsea House Publishers and Gary Tong (artist); from Grumet 1989.

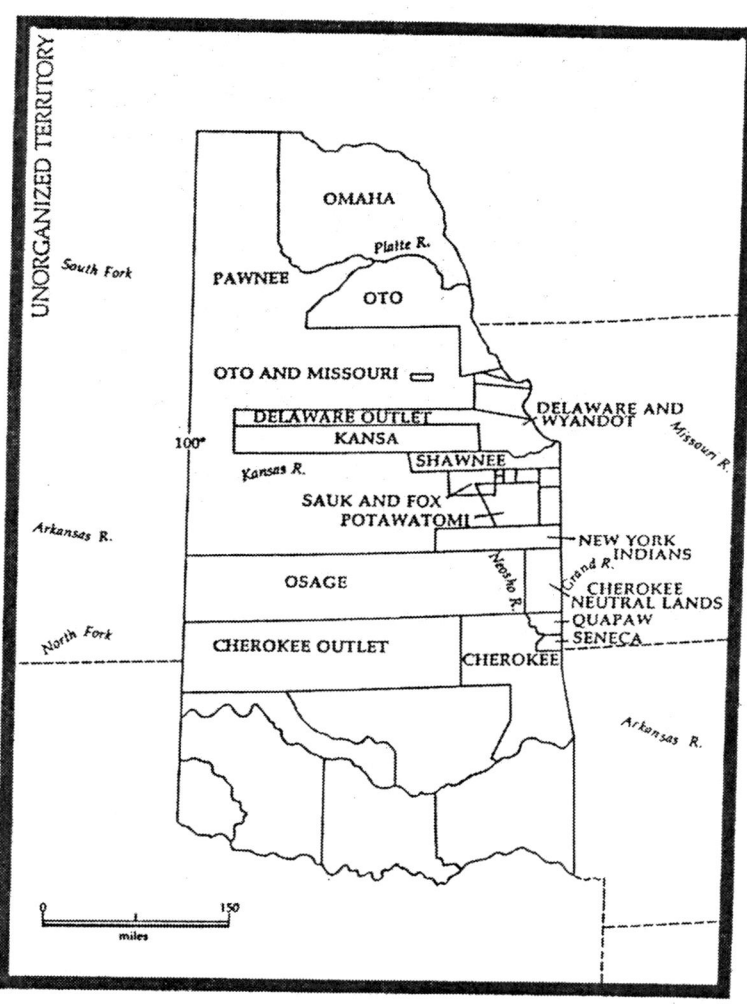

Map 5: Based on Waldman (1985:181). Drawn by Harry Deban.

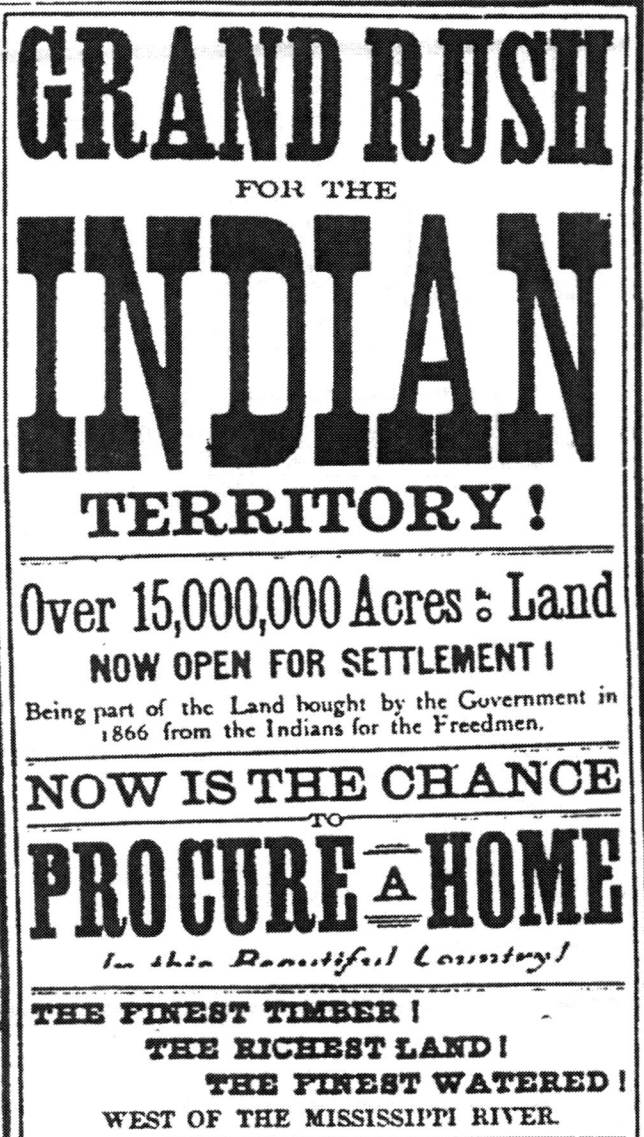

Illustration 6:   Indian Land Ad (taken from Grumet 1989:92). Permission for use granted by the Library of Congress.

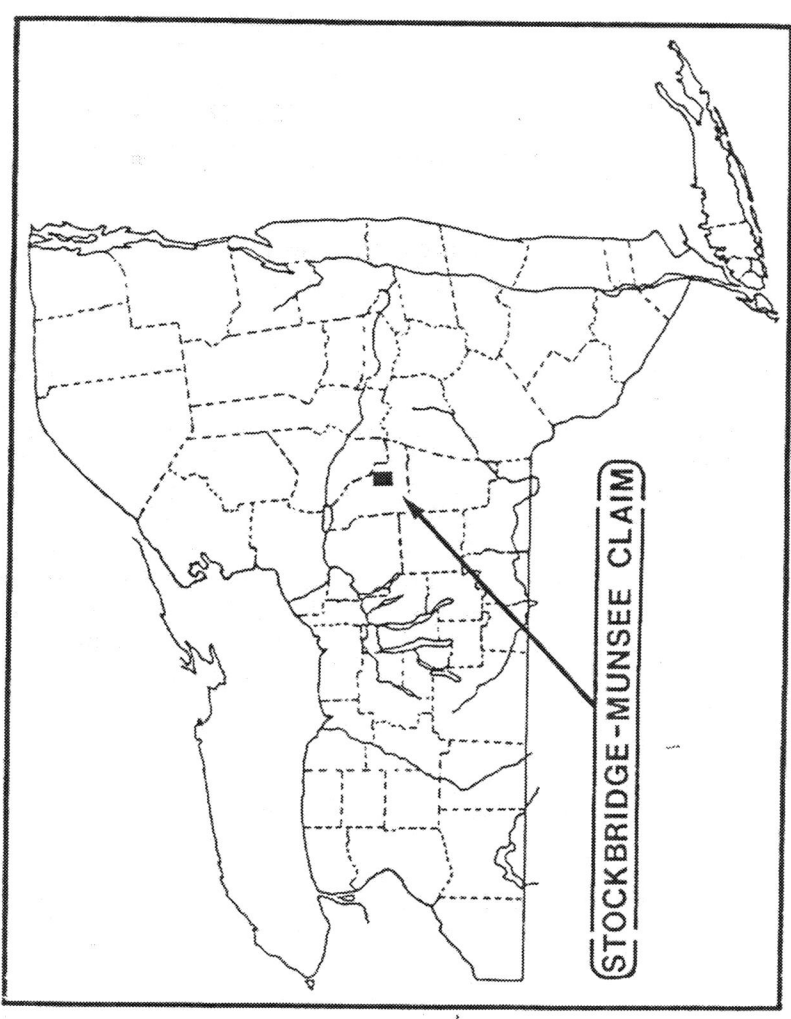

STOCKBRIDGE-MUNSEE CLAIM

Map 7:   Based on map in Vecsey and Starna (1988:4). Revised
          and drawn by Harry Deban.

Chapter 5:

The Stockbridge Munsee Land Claim: A Historical and Legal Perspective

Both the Oneida tribe of Wisconsin and the Stockbridge-Munsee community were plaintiffs in this lawsuit. They both provided evidence to the court of composition and ancestry to the present day petitioners. The Emigrant New York Indians of Wisconsin were organized into two groups: the Oneida tribe of Wisconsin and the Stockbridge-Munsee community (Mochon 1968:195). Both of these groups reside on a reservation established under treaties between the United States and the Menominee tribe that were signed on February 8, 1831 and October 27, 1832.

The removal of the tribe from New York was first discussed in a Six Nations (Iroquois) council meeting in 1810. A formal request was sent to President Madison in 1815. The request by the New York Indians asked the President to approve of the Western relocation of the tribe. The New York Indians also requested that agreements under current treaties and annuity payments continue unchanged.

On February 12, 1816 Secretary of War William H. Crawford advised the chiefs of the Six Nations that the President had granted their request. He noted that the United States government would provide, official backing for the resettlement project and that the government would not permit other tribes to cede lands acquired by the New York Indians. In 1820, an exploratory party left for the Green Bay area in what was then the Michigan Territory. The party was supported by the United States government which provided $300 for equipment and provisions for the ten person party as well as an order that could be used to procure rations at a number of military posts. While this party was in route to Wisconsin, they learned that Colonel Bowyer (the Indian Agent at Green Bay) had purchased the area near Green Bay that they were interested in. Colonel Bowyer had purchased this land from the Menominee. The New York Indians returned to Washington to protest this purchase. Governor Cass, in a letter dated

November 11, 1820 came to their aid. In addition to supporting the non-ratification of the Bowyer purchase he also noted that by doing this the tribe would be bound to the United States, thus ensuring their fidelity. The Governor also viewed the New York Indians as a valuable check against the Winnebagoes which he referred to as the "worst affected of any Indians upon our borders"[1] (ILCCR, 1964:566).The Secretary of War agreed with Governor Cass and the purchase was not ratified.

Once again a party of New York Indians went out to Green Bay. They were assisted by the Secretary of War Calhoun who authorized a loan of $600 from the Bank of Utica to cover their expenses. In addition, he requested assistance from the United States government officers for provisions. Major Biddle, the Green Bay agent, was asked to help the delegation in their negotiations with the Menominees to ensure a successful completion of their expedition.

A treaty was signed on August 18, 1821 in which the Menominee and Winnebago ceded a tract of 804,000 acres. The New York Indians paid $500 as a down payment for the land. In addition they agreed to pay an additional $1,500 within one year of the treaty date. President Monroe approved this treaty on February 19, 1822.

It is interesting to point out that C. Trowbridge had informed Governor Cass that the French inhabitants in the Green Bay area were opposed to this treaty. Once again however, Governor Cass supported the purchase of the land by the New York Indians. In a letter written on October 22,1821 to the Secretary of War Calhoun he once again noted that the New York Indians would form a barrier in this part of the country and that would be "highly useful in the event of any difficulties in that remote quarter" (ILCCR, 1964:569). Once again the Secretary of War agreed with the position of the Governor (Turcheneske 1985:202).

The New York Indians were not satisfied with the land purchased under this treaty due to its distance from Green Bay and the relative small size of the tract. Once again another delegation was formed with the support of the United States government. Governor Cass appointed John Sergeant Jr. to supervise the negotiations.

On September 23, 1822 a treaty was concluded at Green Bay by which the Menominees conveyed to the Stockbridge, Oneida, Tuscarora. St. Regis and Munsee a tract of 7,480,000 acres. The purchase price of this land was a total of $3,000. There was a $1,000 down payment and the balance of $2,000 had to be paid within two years. It is most important to note here that in the 1822 treaty the land cession extended as far south as the Milwaukee River. In later treaties this boundary line between the Menominee and the Chippewas was redrawn. This occurred twice; first at the treaty of Prairie du Chin (August 19, 1825) and then again at the treaty of Butte des Morts {August 11, 1827). The net result of this was that the amount of land ceded in the 1822 treaty decreased from 7,480,000 acres to only 3,931,000 acres. The amount of land purchased by the New York Indians was reduced yet again by a "conditional" approval given to the treaty of September 23, 1822 by President Monroe on March 13, 1823. The net result of this approval resulted in a decrease of the amount of land purchased by the New York Indians to 1,557,000 acres. The President noted in his approval of redrawn boundary lines yet again between the Menomonee and Winnebago that the boundary line of the purchase was to be drawn only to the "head of Sturgeon bay, and no further, that quantity being deemed sufficient for the use of the first before-mentioned tribes and nations of Indians" (ILCCR, 1957:574). The New York Indians protested against this limitation of the 1822 land cession. The Ogden land Company, which owned the pre-exemption rights to the lands owned by the tribe in New York also protested. On October 27, 1823 Secretary of War Calhoun wrote a letter, which is a masterpiece of obfuscation. In the letter he noted that the government sanctioned the amount of land that was "believed to be sufficient for your accommodation" (ILCCR, 1957:575). Later Calhoun really makes himself clear:

> Brothers, Your great father the President wishes you distinctly to understand that he does not mean, by the partial sanction which he has, or may give, to the arrangement between you and the Menomenees, to interfere with, or in any manner invalidate your title to all the lands which you have thereby acquired, including those not confirmed by the government. On the contrary he considers your title to every part of the country conveyed to you by the Menomenees as equally valid against them, and has no objection to your occupying and using the same, as if the whole extent, although it does not think proper to give its special sanction so far, affords sufficient proof that you have not acted without authority, that what you have done has been done with the full assent of the government and that there is nothing which should create dissatisfaction among the Menomenees or your own people to prevent the arrangement as it was originally concluded between you from being carried mutually and faithfully into effect. (ILCCR, 1957:576)

The Emigrant New York Indians did not accept the President's limited approval but instead relied upon their rights under the 1822 treaty with the

Menominees. By 1831, more than six hundred Emigrant New York Indians had moved to Wisconsin at an expense of about $40,000.

It has already been noted that in 1821 at the time of the negotiation and execution of the first treaty between the New York Indians and the Menominees, the French settlers were opposed to the treaty and made an effort to thwart its completion. Trow bridge noted this same French faction opposed the treaty of September 23, 1822. John Sergeant Jr. reported this to Governor Cass in a letter dated September 23, 1822. Col. Pinckney, the commandant at Fort Howard near Green Bay wrote a letter to Eleazer Williams on October 1, 1823 that points out several interesting facts. He noted that in addition to the French settlers attempting to thwart the treaty proceedings, the American Fur Company also had a great interest in preventing the settlement of the area by the Emigrant New York Indians. Col Pinckney stated as follows:

> I learn from good authority that most of the principal claimants here are much involved in debt, and that the American Fur Company has recently taken mortgages of their land to a very considerable amount to be paid in two years. Should they fail to meet this payment their lands fall of course to the Fur Company, when they must make another location and with this view no doubt, will endeavor to prevent the ratification by the Government of your Treaty made with the Menominee Nation last year. (ILCCR, 1957: 581)

The early white settlers in the Green Bay area were of French Extraction. The settlers were engaged in the fur trade with the British and had helped the British both before, during and after the war of 1812. A number of these French settlers had some influence over the Menominee due to intermarriage. Yet another faction of traders and settlers who were using Indian .lands without payment protested against the treaty of September 23, 1822. This protest was supported by two Menominee Chiefs — Oshkosh and Josette. Indian Agent H.B. Brevoort noted in a letter to Governor Cass on July 2, 1824 that he felt that the settlers who were married to or kept Indian women had influenced these two young Menominee Chiefs. He noted that this group (of about 100 people) had established mills near the settlements of the New York Indians. Due to all this potential for conflict with the settlers, the New York Indians petitioned the President for protection from the white Green Bay settlers. The United States Government did provide military protection for the New York Indians against the French settlers and this Menominee faction. Thomas L. McKenney in a letter to Agent Brevoort (dated March 1825) noted that the commanding officer of the Post was ordered to cooperate with you (Agent Brevoort) to provide protection as needed. He said:

> It is very important to preserve peace between the Indians at Green Bay and the New York Indians who may join them, the arrangement between them to this effect having been made with the sanction of the government, gives them a peculiar claim to protection against the acts of designing and intermeddling white men. (ILCCR, 1957:584)

The treaty of Prairie de Chien was signed on August 19, 1825. The Emigrant New York Indians did not participate in this treaty. The purpose of this treaty was to attempt to fix definite boundary lines between the Indian tribes that resided in the State of Wisconsin. Participating tribes included the Sioux, Chippewa, Sac and Fox, Menominee, Ioway, Winnebago, and a portion of the Ottawa Chippewa and Potawattornie. The United States did however recognize the land cession obtained by the Emigrant New York Indians from the Menominees as a part of this treaty. On January 8, 1825 the Brotherton Indians signed a treaty with the Stockbridge, St. Regis, First Christian Party of the Oneida, Tuscaroras and Munsee. As a result of this treaty the Brotherton acquired an interest in the land ceded by the Menominee to the Emigrant New York Indians (Turcheneske 1985:202).The Brotherton then wrote to President Adams requesting that they be allowed to remove to the Green Bay area. They also informed Secretary of War James Barbour that they wished to be allowed to take part in the government treaty council with the Menominee, Winnebago and Chippewa tribes at Green Bay to be held the following summer.

On March 26, 1827 Governor Cass wrote a letter to Colonel McKenney, Commissioner of Indian Affairs. He suggested that a council be held at Green Bay to help settle boundary lines between the Menominee, Winnebagoes and New York Indians, He also noted the interest of the United States Government in this area as follows:

> It would also be proper to provide for distinct boundaries between our settlement upon Fox river and the Indian lands. The subject has been left undefined since the occupation of the Country by the French, and much difficulty has been the consequence. I would also suggest the propriety of adding to our cession here. The country is valuable and would settle; and it is

important to increase the physical strength and resources of that region. (ILCCR, 1957:587)

In August of 1827 Governor Cass and Colonel McKenney held a treaty council at Butte des Mort on the Fox River near Green Bay. Oshkosh and Josette were appointed to represent the Menominee. These were the same two young Menominee Chiefs who opposed the migration of the Emigrant New York Indians into the area. The Menominees and Winnebagoes were represented by Judge Doty, the local land speculator who also was opposed to the claims of the New York Indians. Thus the Emigrant New York Indians had no representatives to speak on their behalf. The treaty was completed on August 11, 1827 and signed by the Chippewa, Menominee and Winnebago. The treaty resulted in three key articles. The first article redrew the boundary line between the Chippewa. Menominee and Winnebagoes. Article two authorized the President to establish a boundary line between the Menominee, Winnebagoes and the Emigrant New York Indians. The third article outlined a tract of land which the Menominee ceded to the United States near Green Bay. Once again the President was allowed to give the final judgment. If he felt that the boundary lines established by the treaty interfered with the claims of the New York Indians then he could adjust them. The quantity of land contained in the tract however could not be larger than the amount defined in the treaty.

In their report to the Secretary of War, Governor Cass and Colonel McKenney noted several key points which can be summarized as follows:

1.   They felt that the United States government was free to take any course it wished in. reference to the 1822 land cession by the Menominees to the Emigrant New York Indians "upon the erroneous ground that the act of acceptance, required by the conditional approval of the President, has not been performed by the New York Indians, and the whole subject is therefore open for examination and decision" (ILCCR, 1957:590).
2.   Once again it was noted that since the Emigrant New York Indians are a farming people they did not requite that much land space.
3.   They also stated that the confirmation of the 1822 treaty "would place beyond the control of the United States the most valuable section of this extensive country" (ILCCR, 1957:590).

The Emigrant New York Indians protested this treaty. The Stockbridge noted that they did not participate in the treaty proceedings and that some of the very same lands which they had received under the 1822 treaty from the Menominee had now been given to the United States under the Treaty of Butte des Morts. The Stockbridge said that if they had been aware of this they would have never sold their land in the east. The Brotherton Indians joined in the Stockbridge protest.

President Adams spoke to Colonel McKenney about the protests of the Stockbridge and Brotherton but did not receive a satisfactory response. He stated " in the instance of the New York Indians removed to Green Bay and of the Cherokees removed to the Territory of Arkansas, we have scarcely given them time to build their wigwams before we are called upon our own people to drive them out again" (ILCCR5, 1957:591). The Senate ratified the treaty on February 19, 1829.

On June 9, 1830 President Jackson appointed Erastus Root, James McCall and John T. Mason as Commissioners to investigate the controversy between the Menominees, Winnebago and New York Indians. Secretary of War Eaton gave these commissioners several very explicit instructions. The commissioners were told to award the New York Indians the smallest possible tract of land. He also informed them that the President had decided to waive any decision in reference to the validity of the treaties of 1821 and 1822.

The Commissioners attempted to obtain the consent of the New York Indians to a vast reduction in the amount of land they had acquired in 1821 and 1822. Although the Stockbridge did not agree, the Commissioners established a boundary line that contained about 300,000 acres for the Stockbridge/Brotherton.

The Commissioners also questioned the validity of the 1822 treaty on two grounds. First they noted that all Chiefs did not sign the treaty. Second, the Commissioners felt that the Menominee never intended to sell their lands but only to permit the Emigrant New York Indians to reside among them. Both of these statements can be refuted. The fact that the tribe divided the payments they received among the entire nation illustrates that this treaty was recognized by the entire nation. Also the treaty of 1827 gave power to the President to confirm the boundaries between the Menominee and the New York Indians. This very act confirmed that the New York Indians had indeed been ceded the land under the previous treaty of 1822.

After a review of the facts, the Commissioners conceded that the treaties of 1821 and 1822 were valid so they then went on to justify the distribution of land that they recommended. Due to their explicit instructions from the War Department, plus the fact that the New York Indians as agriculturists supposedly did not need that much land, the Commissioners decided to award the New York Indians with a 300,000 acre tract of land while granting the Menominees five or six million acres. Once again they left the President to serve as the final judge regarding the 1821 and 1822 treaties.

On February 8, 1831 the Stambaugh Treaty was completed between the United States and the Menominee despite the objections of the New York Indians. The key provisions of this treaty were as follows:

1. The Emigrant New York Indians lost all of the land rights they had acquired at Green Bay and most of the land they had purchased in the 1821 and 1822 treaties.
2. The Menominees ceded 500,000 acres of land to the United States which was to be reserved for the New York Indians.
3. 100 acres of this land was to be given to each New York Indian who relocated to this area with the balance of the surplus land reverting to the United States.
4. The United States agreed to pay the Menominees §20,000 for the cession that was allocated for the New York Indians.
5. The third article of the treaty required the Menominees to cede to the United States 2.5 million acres of land east of Winnebago Lake in the Green Bay area.   A good portion of this land had been sold before to the New York Indians and approved by President Monroe in 1823.

The Stambaugh Treaty was brought before the Senate Committee on Indian Affairs on February 28, 1831. Secretary of War Eaton, in a letter to the President noted that the treaties of 1821 and 1822 were not valid because they were not ratified by the Senate. He went on to state that "it did not occur to me as proper to present the demand of the New York Indians as a matter resting upon right and justice" (ILCGR, 1957:599). The Senate however, adjourned without further action on the treaty.

In the fall of 1831 the Emigrant New York Indians sent a delegation to protest the ratification of the Stambuagh Treaty. The new Secretary of War Cass appointed the new Governor of Michigan, C.S. Porter, to meet with the delegates. Governor Porter did not reach a compromise with the New York Indian delegation and instead recommended that the Senate ratify the treaty noting the interest in the United States in promoting White settlement of the Green Bay area.

The Stambaugh Treaty was ratified by the Senate on June 25, 1832 with some amendments that changed the location of lands set aside for the New York Indians. Two townships on the east side of Winnebago Lake were given to the Stockbridge-Munsee. Another township was given to the Brotherton. The Stockbridge-Munsee tract, was 46,080 acres while the

Brotherton township was 23,040 acres. Another 500,000 acres was set aside for all the remaining New York Indians who choose to emigrate to the area subject to diminution. It must be noted that this total of 569,120 acres was even less then the amount of land acquired by the New York Indians under the 1821 treaty with the Menominees and Winneaboes. The effect of the treaties of 1831 and 1832 was to deprive the Emigrant New York Indians of all the lands conveyed to them under their 1822 treaty with the Menominees. The Emigrant New York Indians consented to this treaty only because of great pressure with the final threat that they would be removed from the Wisconsin area if they did not accept the terms offered to them.

The Treaty of Buffalo Creek signed on January 15, 1838 between the United States and the New York Indians left in New York state required the tribe to relinquish to the United States all rights to the lands ceded to them by the Menominee Treaty of 1831 except for a small tract of land upon which the New York Indians who had already moved to Green Bay were living on. In return the United States gave the tribe 1,824,000 in Kansas as a permanent home for all New York Indians. On February 3, 1838 another treaty was completed between the United States and the Oneida Indians residing in Green Bay. In this treaty, the Oneida ceded all lands given to them by the Menominee in the treaties of 1831 and 1832. In return the United States paid the Orchard Party Oneidas $3,000 and the First Christian Party $30,500. The Oneida were also given a 65,000 acre reservation in Wisconsin.

The Stockbridge-Munsee by a treaty on November 24, 1848 were paid $25,000 by the United States in return for their release of all claims to lands in Indian and Wisconsin. This amount was paid out over a ten-year period in irregularly spaced installments of $5,000. The rest of the Emigrant New York Indians were not compensated for loss of the lands wrongfully taken by the United States which had been ceded to them by treaties in 1831 and 1832. The United States did not live up to its two former promises to acknowledge title to lands obtained by the Emigrant New York Indians and to protect any lands obtained so that they could not be granted away. In fact, while pretending to serve as an arbitrator between the Menominee and the Emigrant New York Indians, the United States instead entered into a separate deal to purchase the disputed lands from the Menominee while excluding the New York Indians from participation. The government clearly failed to serve as a guardian in this case but acquired the lands purchased by the Emigrant New York Indians in 1822 instead for its own profit. There can be no question that the United States violated the standards of fair and honorable dealings with respect to the Emigrant New York Indians.

Legal Commentary

The Stockbridge-Munsee filed a series of claims with the Indian Claims Commission from the late 1950s through the early 1960s. These claims involved lands ceded by the tribe in Wisconsin and Michigan. The Commission upheld the claims, and after appeals and congressional action, the tribe was awarded a monetary settlement.

In the *Supplemental Findings of Fact* {11 Ind. Cl. Comm. 336), decided on October 8, 1962, the Commission elaborated on how it had reached a value for the area claimed by the tribe. Great care was taken to describe geography and natural resources of the area in question. Earlier cases had decided that the Stockbridge and other related groups had in fact a valid claim. This procedure was done to determine the value of the land.

The Commission recounted the early exploration and migration into the claimed area by European and later by Americans. The natural resources such as rivers and timber were reviewed in great detail. Based on the economic value of the land in question, a price per acre was established. The Commission acknowledged that the plaintiff had a undivided interest in half the 4,037,000 acres being claimed in 1832, when the wrong occurred. This interest was based on treaty obligations and federally arranged purchases from other tribes in the claimed area. After making certain deductions allowed by law for past compensation received by the tribe (known as "offsets" }, the Commission based an award on the fair market value of the land in 1832, This seems somewhat absurd to the outside observer considering that the Stockbridge had to wait over a century to obtain the money owed to them for the lands taken. One would think that they would at least receive interest on the money. This was not the case. Like so many other tribes who won awards in the court, the money owed from a century before was paid. However, at 19th-century values it came to late to benefit those it should have been paid to and was too little to truly help those who received it in this century.

Today the Stockbridge remain a poor tribe on a equally poor reservation. The system used by the Indian Claims Commission which acknowledged valid tribal claims in exchange for only paying the amount due at the time the wrong was committed allowed the United States government to pay the claims rather cheaply. With no interest due and often 19th-century land values used, the tribes did not receive what was truly due them.

REFERENCES

ILCCR (= Indian Land Claims Commission Reports)
   1957 Docket 75, Volume 5:594-635. Washington: United States
   Government Printing Office.
   1962 Docket 75, Volume 11:336-386. Washington: United States
   Government Printing Office.
   1964 Docket 75, Volume 13-.560-573C. Washington: United States
   Government Printing Office.

Mochon, Marion Johnson
   1988 Stockbridge-Munsee Cultural Adaptation. *Procedings of the
   American Philosophical Society* 112:182-218.

Turchensek, John Jr.
   1985 Federal Indian Policy and the Brotherton Indians. Pp. 201-209
   in *Papers of the Sixteenth Algonquian Conference.* William Cowan,
   ed. Ottawa: Carleton University.

Chapter 6:

Delaware Participation
in the American Civil War

A total of 170 Delaware Indians volunteered for service in the Union Army during the American Civil War. The Commissioner of Indian Affairs reported in 1862 that of a total of 210 Delaware adult males between the ages of 18 and 45, 170 had volunteered for the Union Army. He added "it is doubtful if any community can show a larger portion of volunteers than this" (Weslager 1972:416).

Of these 170 Delawares we have found records of a total of 32 who participated in two volunteer regiments of Kansas Cavalry: Company E of the 15th and Company M of the 6th. Company E, of the 15th volunteer Kansas Cavalry included six Delawares: Doctor Black, Thomas Lewis, Wilson Sar-coxie, Charles W. Ketchum, Big Moccasin, and George Pempsey (Weslager 1972: 416). Company M of the 6th volunteer Cavalry included a total of 26 Delawares including: Sgt. William R. Ketchum, Benjamin Wright, Solomon Love, Joseph W. Love, Yellow Leaf, Thomas Wilson, Joseph Sarcoxie, John Fish, Jacob Linneas, John Hatt, Jacob Hill, John File, George Cummings, John Shawnee, Alex J. Conner, John JourneyCake, John B. Pascal, Young Bobb, Young Jim, Benjamin Journeycake, Byan Washington, Samuel Wise, Philip Brokenknife, John Bill, John Capps, and James Partridge (Weslager 1972: Appendix 9:514).

Historical Context

There are several notes pertaining to the formation and recruitment of the Delaware Indians into the Union Army in the historical record (Gibson 1985:390). In a letter from Albert Pike dated May 26, 1861, he notes the formation of a battalion including Delawares:

You will make known to the Delawares, and if practicable to the Kickapoos, that it is my desire, and I have authority, to enlist a battalion of 350 men, of the Delawares, Kickappos, and Shawnees. I shall be greatly obliged to you for all assistance you can render in securing the services in aims of the Kickapoos and the Delawares.   They will be paid like other mounted men, receiving 40 cents a day for use and risk of their horse, in addition to their pay, rations and clothing will be provided, (Abel 1992:181)

There is also another note from a letter to the Indian Agent of the Delaware requesting Falleaf to organize a party of 50 Delawares for service in the Union Army (Abel 1992:480).

Josephy (1991:330) has noted that "Pike's treaties had set the stage for a Indian 'little civil war[1] that forced the people within each tribe to choose sides in the larger conflict." Many loyal Indian families fled North to Union-held Kansas. For the Delaware, a total of 170 men ended up volunteering for the Union Army.

Josephy (1991:354) has noted that there were several reasons why Lincoln allowed Native Americans to serve in the Union Army.

1.   the general shortage of troops in the West
2.   support of the idea by General Hunter and William P. Dole (Commissioner of Indian Affairs).
3.   confederates use of Indians at the battle of Pea Ridge
4.   The desire of many Indian refugees in Kansas to help retake their lands in Indian Territory

The Delaware were also induced to fight for economic reasons — the Union pay of 40 cents per day, and cultural reasons — the male need to prove themselves in battle (Alexander 1992:54).

Activities of the Delaware Units

The 15th Kansas Cavalry

The 15th Kansas Cavalry began Federal Service at Ft. Leavenworth in September of 1863. The Delaware fought in Company E. "The 15th Kansas Cavalry spent its entire Career in the Departments of Missouri and Kansas (Walters 1993: 1). At various times the regiment's companies were stationed at Fort Leavenworth, Olathe, Paoli, Coldwater Grove, Trading Post, Fort Scott, Osage Mission, and Hurnbold Kansas. The 15th Kansas Cavalry took part in a number of engagements during its career. These are identified below. These engagements included (Walters 1992:2):

skirmish, Clear Creek, Missouri (May 16, 1864)

scout from Fort Leavenworth Kansas (1) to Weston, Missouri (2) June 13-16, 1864

expedition from Fort Leavenworth, Kansas (1) to Farley, Missouri (3) June 16-20, 1864

operations against Price's Invasion of Missouri (Sept. 29 to Nov. 3, 1864)

action, Lexington, Missouri (4) (Oct. 19, 1864)

action, Little Blue, Missouri (5) (Oct. 21, 1864)

action, Independence, Missouri (6) (Oct. 22, 1864)

action, Byram's Ford, Big Blue, State Line, Missouri (7) (Oct. 22, 1864)

engagement, Westport (8), Big Blue (7), Missouri (Oct. 23, 1864)

skirmish, Coldwater Grove, Missouri (Oct. 24, 1864)

battle, Manniton (Chariot), Missouri (9) (Oct. 25, 1864)

engagement, Mine Creek, Little Osage River, Marias des Cygiies, Kansas (10) (Oct. 25, 1864)

engagement, Newtionia, Missouri (11) (Oct. 28, 1864)

The regiment continued to serve at various locations for the remainder of its career. In early October 1865, all of the companies (except Company H) were concentrated at Fort Leavenworth, They were mustered out of Federal service there on October 19, 1865. Company H was mustered out at Fort Riley on December 7, 1865 (Walters 1993:3).

During its career the 15th Kansas Cavalry sustained the loss of two officers and 19 enlisted men killed or mortally wounded. An additional two officers and 77 enlisted men died from disease or other non- battlefield causes (Walters 1993:3).

The 6th Kansas Volunteer Cavalry

Delaware who participated in Company M of the 6th Kansas Volunteer Cavalry spent their entire time in the Arkansas theater. They were involved in four engagements of note:

Steel's Expedition from Little Rock, Arkansas (38) to Camden (39), Arkansas (March 23 to May 3, 1864)

action, Moscow, **Arkansas** (42) (April 13, 1864)

skirmishes and engagement Camden, Arkansas (39) (April 16-18, 1864)

engagement at, Jenkins Ferry (44) Saline River, Arkansas (April 30, 1864)

The following is a selection of letters of the 6th Kansas Cavalry from the field:

(1)   From the camp of the Sixth Kansas, April 20, 1864:

COLONEL; I have the honor to submit the following report: On the 17th of April, 1864, 1 was detailed with 25 men belonging to the different companies of the Sixth Regiment Kansas Cavalry, for the purpose of re-enforcing Colonel Williams. My men were in the advance of the force sent out and were continually skirmishing with the enemy after leaving our pickets until going into camp for the night. We saw at no time more than 50 of the enemy. We went into camp about 10 miles from Camden. Sent to Colonel Williams to know if we should advance. He said for us to remain. During the night our camp was not disturbed. The following morning moved two miles farther and remained until the train had passed, when Colonel Williams detailed 20 of my men to go 2 miles on the Washington road as escort to ten wagons for the purpose of getting corn. While on this duty the fight commenced. I then had the rest of my men go into the timber of the right of the road as the skirmishers in rear of the train. They soon came back and reported a regiment of infantry and two pieces of artillery immediately in front of them. Our cavalry then formed on the right of the Eighteenth Iowa Regiment and remained until the colored regiment and section of Rabbs battery had been routed and fallen back to the rear of the train.

I was then ordered by Colonel Williams to form what men I had and assist his men. that were wounded to get away, if possible, during which time my men acted as well as men could act under the circumstances; for the enemy were following the negroes and pouring a heavy fire into their ranks until sheltered by the timber. I remained with Colonel Williams and his men until we arrived at Camden. I am satisfied that the train was surrounded cm three sides before the fight commenced. The two pieces of artillery on the || right of the road at the rear of the train were not used by the enemy during | the engagement. I lost no men from my command. Respectfully, yours

R.L. Phillips,
Second Lieut Company C, Sixth Kansas Vol Cavalry
(Walters 1993:31} J

(2)   Camp near Camden, April 20, 1864:

COLONEL; I would respectfully report the part taken by a section of howitzers attached to the Sixth Regiment Kansas Volunteer Cavalry in an engagement with the enemy on the 18th instant: First, number of commissioned officers present 1; number of enlisted men, 24.   Second, Private Christopher C Goodman, Company D, Sixth Kansas Volunteer Cavalry, and attached to and doing duty with a section of artillery attached to the Sixth Kansas Volunteer Cavalry, was killed in the early part of the engagement. Private Henry Gabie, Company K, Sixth Kansas Volunteer Cavalry, and attached to and doing duty with a section of howitzer attached to the Six Kansas Volunteer Cavalry, is missing, supposed to be a prisoner. Third, I was ordered with my command, in conjunction with the Eighteenth

Infantry and detachments of the Second, Sixth, and Fourteenth Kansas Cavalry, all under command of Capt Duncan, of Eighteenth Iowa Infantry, to reinforce the escort of the forage train under command of Colonel Williams, First Kansas Colored Infantry, and proceeded with them to camp, about 12 miles from Camden.

I brought the section into battery three times on the march, our cavalry skirmishing nearly all the way to camp. I did not fire a shot, it not being necessary. On the morning of the 18th. I moved on with the command until we met the train, distant about 13 miles. I then, after the train had passed, took my position in rear with the rear guard and moved a short distance when firing commenced in front. I took my position three times on the right of the road, facing to the front, but was each time ordered farther to the right. I was then ordered to fall back of the left of the road, facing to the left. I remained there until our forces commenced falling back in disorder, when I *was* ordered to fall back to the hill in our rear, when I remained until ordered to retreat, the enemy pouring in a heavy fire from our right. I did so, and fell back about one-quarter of a mile, when we came to a creek where it was impossible to get the guns over, and I was obliged to abandon the guns, spiking while under a severe fire of the enemy. The men under my command behaved well.

I remain, colonel, very respectfully, your obedient servant,

AJ Walker
First Lieut Comdg Howitzer Detachment, Sixth Kansas Vol Cav. (Walters 1993:31-33)

Black Beaver and Captain Falleaf

A United States Senate Document from the 61st Congress, document 134 has some information and letters from two Delaware who distinguished themselves in the Civil War, Black Beaver and Captain Falleaf. Black Beaver served in both the Mexican and the Civil War as a Scout. Black Beaver also served as a guide for naturalist John J. Audubon.

In a letter dated September 25,1863, Indian Agent Johnson stated that "One-half of the adult population (of the Delaware) are in the volunteer service of the United States. They make the best soldiers and are highly esteemed by their officers. The tribe has shown their devotion and loyalty to the Government by the number of men furnished to the army."

John Conner a head Chief of the Delaware wrote to O-PUTH-LA-YAR-HO-LA, Musogee Chief Warrior:

We are much rejoiced to receive your letter by James McDaniels and David Balon. Our agent has sent it to our Great Father, the President at Washington, and to General Hunter at Fort Leavenworth. It gives us great pleasure to hear that you are good and true friends to the President and to the Government of the United States. We hope you will continue to be their friends. If bad men of the South ask you to go to war against the President stop your ears; don't listen to them; they are your worst enemies; they are trying to destroy you and the country. (US Senate Document 134:12)

Black Beaver also wrote a letter that discusses his service in the Civil War:

Dear Sir: I take the liberty of addressing my grievances to you and of respectfully asking your advice in a matter in which 1 am earnestly concerned.

I would represent that I am an Indian, belonging to the Delaware tribe. That I have been in the employ of the Government all or nearly all of the time since the commencement of the Mexican war. During the Mexican war I was captain of a company of Shawnees and Delawares in the United States Army.

Since that time, up to the commencement of the last war, I have been employed as guide or interpreter by the different commanding officers at the posts of Arbuckle and Fort Cobb, in the Indian Territory, and by superintendent and agents for the Indians in the vicinity of Fort Cobb and Arbuckle, as can be attested by Generals Marcy, Emery, Sturgies, Stantly, and Sacklitt, any or all of the military officers stationed at the aforenamed posts prior to the war, as also ex- Superintendent Rector, of Arkansas, and all of the United States Indian agents in that locality.

I was at the post of Fort Arbuckel for about five years and the post of Fort Cobb one year immediately preceding the last war, and during that time had invested all of my means and earnings in cattle and hogs, and had at the breaking out of the war a large stock of cattle and hogs, as will be attested by some, if not all, of the aforenamed persons.

In the spring of 1861 General Emery requested me to guide his command and also the combined commands from Forts Smith, Cobb, and Arbuckel to Fort Leavenworth, Kansas, which I did, but hesitated about leaving my stock until General Emery assured me that I should be paid by the United States for my losses, and on that representation I complied with his request and came with his command to Fort Leavenworth Kansas, and remained there until the war ceased. When I visited my old place and found that my stock was killed, some having been destroyed by the wild Indians and some by ths Southern Army. (US Senate Document 134:14)

Black Beaver goes on in his letter to request payment for his livestock that was destroyed while he was employed by the United States Government.

Another letter from Indian Agent Johnson notes that James Ketchum raised a company of half-breed Delawares to report to Fort Leavenworth and be mustered as Kansas volunteers (US Senate Document 134:15).

Major General Jas. G. Blunt noted in a letter dated January 25, is that the Delaware Indians participated in the First and Second Regiment of the Indian Home Guards that, were organized in the spring of 1862. He noted that six companies of Delawares as well as Osages were accepted and mustered into the Second Regiment {US Senate Document 134:20).

In a letter Captain Falleaf noted that he headed several companies of Delaware soldiers during the Civil War. The first was organized in the fall of 1861 at the request of Major-General Fremont. There were 54 Delawares in this company. In the summer of 1862 Captain Falleaf served under Colonel Ritchie of Topeka, Kansas and fought in an engagement near Fort Gibson. In this case Captain Falleaf had a company of 86 Delawares that served under Colonel Ritchie for five months. He also noted in his letter that neither he nor any of his men had received pay for their services (US Senate Document 134:16).

In a letter Major-General W.H. Emory noted the excellent service of Black Beaver:

> GENERAL; I have read carefully the letters of Black Beaver, the Delaware guide, dated Baxter Springs Kansas, June 3, 1869, and I hereby certify that it is every word true. And I exceedingly regret that the Government has so far neglected the claim of this worthy and patriotic man who has rendered such eminent and valuable service.

> When the war broke out, I was in quasi command of the troops in the Indian country, on the northern frontier of Texas; that is to say, I was to take command and withdraw the troops only in case Arkansas passed the act of succession. She never passed that act before proceeding to actual hostilities and to the attempt to capture the troops stationed in the Indian country, so that when I got information of what was going on I was obliged to act without orders from the Government, Orders subsequently arrived, but not until long after the steps were taken which I now describe, and in which Black Beaver rendered such splendid service.

> That step was to concentrate all the troops at Arbuckle and withdraw them in mass. Before the concentration could be effected,

I learned from undoubted authority that 4,000 rebels from Texas were marching directly on me and that some 2,000 from Arkansas were moving to strike my flank.

This compelled me to seek, with my comparatively small command, the open prairie. To do this, guides were essential, and of all the Indians upon whom the Government had been lavishing its bounty Black Beaver was the only one that would consent to guide my column.

He was living near Fort Arbuckel, in a comfortable house, surrounded by his family, with a small farm well stocked with cattle and horses and a field of corn. All of these he abandoned to serve the United States, with a full knowledge that in doing so his horses and cattle would be seized by the enemy and his property destroyed, and such was the case: and Black Beaver has never returned to his home, and it is my belief if he was now to return he would be murdered by the bad white men who in 1861 instigated the Indians to go into rebellion against the United States, and who he so greatly offended by guiding my command through the prairie in safety to Fort Leavenworth.

I need not say how invaluable was his services and great his sacrifice on that occasion. He was the first to warn me of the approach of the enemy and give me the information by which I was enabled to capture the enemy's advance guard—the first prisoners captured in the war.

I can not too urgently press upon the honorable commissioner the justice of this claim and the pressing necessity there is for doing something at once to relieve the wants of this aged and worthy man.

I have the honor to be, yours, respectfully

WH Emory, Brevet Major-General US Army to General ES Parker (Commissioner of Indian Affairs). (US Senate Document 134:24, 25)

Conclusion

The goal of this brief paper has been to illustrate the participation of the Delaware in the Civil War. There has been very little written in the historical record on the contributions of Algonquian Indian tribes and their participation in this war. The only real exception to this is a new book by Hauptman (1993) on the Iroquois in the Civil War. Certainly the contributions of the Delaware who fielded a total of 170 males for the Union Army should not be totally overlooked. We hope this paper has done a small amount to point out this otherwise overlooked contribution.

REFERENCES

Abel, Annie Heloise
  1992 *The American Indian in the Civil War.* Lincoln : University of
  Nebraska Press,
  1992 *The American Indian as Slaveholder and Secessionist.* Lincoln:
  University of Nebraska Press.

 Alexander, Ted
  1992 Muskets and Tomahawks. *Civil War Magazine* 10:8-15.
  Gibson, Arrell Morgan
  1985 Native Americans in the Civil War. *American Indian Quartly*
  9:385-410.

Hauptman, Laurence M.
  1993 *The Iroquois in the Civil War From Battle Field to Reservation.*
  Syracuse-|: Syracuse University Press.

Josephy, Alvin M., Jr.
  1991 *The Civil War* in *the American West.* New York: Alfred A. Knopf.

United States Senate Document
  1909 No. 134. Pp. **12-16 and** 24-25. 61st Congress, 1st Session, US
  Senate: Washington.

Walters, John
  1993 History of the 6th Kansas **Volunteer** Cavalry. Institute for Civil
  War

Research. Ms.
  1993 History of the 15th Kansas Volunteer Cavalry. Institute for Civil
  War Research. Ms.

Westlager, C.A.
  1972 *The Delaware Indians: A History.* New Brunswick, NJ: Rutgers
  University Press.

Chapter 7:

Black Beaver

Black Beaver (Suck-tum-mah-kway) was born in Belleville, Illinois in 1806, the son of a Delaware chief, Captain Patterson (Nichols and Hauptman 1997:38).

In 1834, when he was 28 years old. Black Beaver served as an interpreter for Colonel Richard Irving Dodge at his conference with the Comanche, Kiowa and Wichita on the upper Red River (Foreman 1946:269). Dodge later wrote of Black Beaver and his people:

of all the Indians, the Delawares seem to be most addicted to these solitary wanderings, undertaken in their case at feast, from pure curiosity and love of adventure... Black Beaver, the friend and guide of General (then Captain) iMarcy, was almost as equally renowned for his wonderful journeys.   [Dodge 1882:554-5]

Dodge was here comparing Black Beaver with John Conner, head chief of the Delaware.

Foreman (1946:262) noted that in the Dragon expedition of 1834 led by General Henry Leavenworth there was a total of 32 Indians including six Delaware; among them was Black Beaver.

During the war with Mexico, from 1846 to 1848, Black Beaver was the captain of a company of about 20 Delaware and 35 Shawnee Indians (Foreman 1946:270). The company was officially known as Black Beaver's Spy Company, Indian, Texas Mounted Volunteers. After the war ended Black Beaver served the army as a scout (Nichols and Hauptman 1997:38).

In April 1849, Captain Randolph B. Marcy was ordered to lead 500 immigrants to California; Black Beaver was engaged as a guide and interpreter. Marcy stated:

> He has traveled a great deal among the western and northern tribes of Indians, is well acquainted with the Character and habits and converses fluently with the Comanche and most of the other prairie tribes. He has spent five years in Oregon and California, two years among the Crow and Black Feet Indians. Has trapped beaver in the Gila, the Columbia, the Rio Grande, and the Pecos; has crossed the Rocky Mountains at many different points, and indeed is one of those men that are seldom met with except in the Mountains. [Marcy 1849:173-4]

For ten years during the 1830s and 1840s Black Beaver had worked for the American Fur Company; after the decline of the Rocky Mountain fur trade, he served as a guide for wagon trains heading west (Nichols and Hauptman 1997:37-38).

In the 1850s Black Beaver functioned as a guide and interpreter at forts Arbuckle and Cobb. In 1858, he served as a guide for Douglas Cooper, the Federal agent for the Chickasaw. Nichols and Hauptman (1977:37) note that Black Beaver "reportedly spoke English, French, Spanish, and about eight different Indian languages, and could also use Plains Indian sign language."

Black Beaver in War Correspondence

Black Beaver's name appears in Union Army correspondence relating to operations in Louisiana and the trans-Mississippi states and territories from January to March, 1864. A letter from Major General John Pope to Brigadier General A. Sully discusses the need to employ as many Shawnee and Delaware as possible in the war effort:

> General: I received yesterday your letter of the 21st. In reply, it is only necessary to say that you will see from General Halleck's endorsement that 1 am authorized to employ (not enlist) such Indians as I may think judicious for service in your campaign. If you remember, we had a conversation on the subject when you were here, and you suggested substantially the plan you now do in your letter, in which I fully agree with you. My idea is to employ as many Shawnees and Delawares, as well as other

Indians who are available, giving them blankets &c. as you suggest, and also what rations they absolutely need, then promising them all the spoils of the campaign, I think in this way you can get for little or nothing some of the very best fighting Indian material on the frontier.

You have my authority to do this to the extent you think judicious. We must by all means make a clean sweep of hostile Indians this summer, as far at least as the "Crow country" and you must employ all the friendly Indians who may be useful for this purpose. I have no doubt you can get many of the Rees and Mandans simply for the privilege of accompanying you in this war and sharing the spoils. This whole matter I leave to your discretion, with the understanding that I will authorize and support every arrangement you think judicious. We must end Indian hostilities this season. I have applied for an engineer officer to report to you with necessary surveying instruments. I have ordered it to accompany the troops Sibley sends from Minnesota. Do you wish to go sooner?

Very truly yours, Jno. Pope, Major-General Commanding. [Civil War CD/ROM 1996]

A second letter from Pope to Sully emphasizes the importance of securing the aid of Black Beaver in employing the Delaware and Shawnee in the war effort: "General: I would suggest to you, in employing Delawares and Shawnees that you send up and secure Black Beaver, who is now somewhere in Kansas" (Civil War CD/ROM 1996).

Another piece of Union correspondence illustrates the high regard with which Black Beaver was held by the Union government and also notes his involvement with a conference with the "Great Father" in Washington. The following letter was sent to Tusaquach, chief of the Wichitas:

Friend and Brother: It is the wish of the commissioner of the United States Government that you either come to Kansas with your friends the Seminoles or send two or three of your best braves. We also want the Keechies, Ionies, Cadoes, and the Commanches to send some of their men to meet and have a talk with the commissioners of your Great Father at Washington. His soldiers are as swift as the antelope and brave as the mountain bear, and they are your friends and brothers. They will give you powder and lead. They will fight by your sides. Your friend Black Beaver will meet you here, and we will drive away the bad men who entered your company last spring. The Texans have killed the Wichitas; we will punish the Texans. Come with your friends the Seminoles. Your brother, E. H. Carruth, Commissioner for the U.S. Government. [Civil War CD/ROM 1996]

Black Beaver's name also appears in Confederate correspondence. A letter to Brigadier General William Steele, Choctaw Nation, notes that Black Beaver was on the Texas frontier in 1863:

Sir: There have been two Caddo Indians from Fort Bent, on the Arkansas, visiting the Reserve Indians now camped on the Washita, near Fort Arbuckle. They brought messages from the Federal Officer in Command, and from the Chiefs of all the bands which left the reserve last year, viz., that they would he down this fait, and would give the Reserve Indians protection, and would have sufficient white force to hold and occupy the country. These messengers were from the band of Jim Pockmark, Caddo, and Anadarko chief. This is no idle rumor and requires immediate attention from the Government, or the frontier of Texas will be ravaged and the Indian Territory overrun. It is said that Jesse Chisolm and Black Beaver are with them. Yours, respectfully. C. B. Johnson. [Civil War | CD/ROM 1996]

In 1862, Black Beaver wrote a letter to the commissioner of Indian Affairs that discusses his service in the Civil War as well as some of his activities as a scout:

Dear Sir: I take the liberty of addressing my grievance to you and of respectfully asking your advice in a matter in which I am earnestly concerned. I would represent that I am an Indian, belonging to the Delaware tribe. That I have been in the employ of the Government all or nearly all of the time since the commencement of the Mexican war. During the Mexican war I was captain of a company of Shawnees and Delawares in the United States Army.

Since that time, up to the commencement of the last war, I have been employed as guide or interpreter by the different commanding officers at the posts of Arbuckle and Fort Cobb, in the

Indian Territory, and by superintendents and agents for the Indians in the vicinity of Fort Cobb and Arbuckle, as can be attested
by Generals Marcy, Emery, Sturgies, Stantly, and Sacklitt, any
or all the military officers stationed at the aforenamed posts
prior to the war, as also ex-Superintendent Rector, of Arkansas,
and all of the United States Indian agents in that locality.

I was at the post of Fort Arbuckle for about five years and the
post of Fort Cobb one year immediately preceding the last war,
and during that time had invested all of my means and earnings
in cattle and hogs, and had at the breaking out of the war a large
stock of cattle and hogs, as will be attested by some, if not all,
of the aforenamed persons.

In the spring of 1861 General Emery requested me to guide his
command and also the combined commands from Forts Smith,
Cobb and Arbuckle to Fort Leavenworth, Kansas, which 1 did,
but hesitated about leaving my stock until General Emery
assured me that I should be paid by the United States for my
losses, and on that representation I complied with his request
and came with his command to Fort Leavenworth, Kansas, and
remained there until the war ceased. When I visited my oid
place and found that my stock was killed, some having been
destroyed by the wild Indians and some by the Southern Army.
[U.S. Senate 1909:13-14]

In 1872 Black Beaver filed a claim with the government for his property on the Washita River which he had abandoned in 1861 and which was
destroyed by Confederates. He valued the property at $22,268. The com-
mittee on Indian affairs recommended a payment of $5000, less than a
quarter of his claim (Foreman 1946:285). The Hon. William G. Donna, of
Iowa, a member of the committee on military affairs, wrote the following
report:

Claimant, a Delaware Indian, was a captain in the United States
Army in the Mexican war; since which time, until the rebellion,
he resided in the Indian Territory, near Fort Arbuckle, and has
frequently been employed by the different commanding officers
at Forts Cobb and Arbuckle, to act as guide and interpreter, in
1861 his means were invested in a farm, well stocked, where he
then resided.

General Emory, then in command of the U.S. troops in that section of the country, learning that the rebels were marching directly upon him, urged claimant to act as guide, to enable him with the combined commands of Forts Smith, Cobb, and Arbuckle, to elude the enemy, and, by seeking the open prairies, to reach Leavenworth Kansas. He (Emory) states that, "of all the Indians upon whom the Government has lavished its bounty, Black Beaver was the only one that would consent to guide the column." To do so he abandoned his property, which appears to have been seized and destroyed by the enemy.

The command reached Leavenworth in safety, and several officers certify to the great value of his services and his unflinching patriotism. He states that he is now over sixty years of age, too feeble to earn a livelihood, and what is justly due him from the Government is all he has to depend on in his old days. [U.S. House of Representatives 1873:278]

Black Beaver was never paid for the livestock destroyed while he was employed by the United States government;

Until his death, in 1880, Black Beaver attempted without success to secure compensation for the sizable losses — estimated at about $5,000 — he had suffered while in Federal service. Well into the 1880s, his daughter, Lucy Pruner, was still trying in vain to collect the monetary damages promised her father more than 25 years before. [Nichols and Hauptman 1997:38]

Conclusion

It is clear from this brief account of Black Beaver's life that he was an important Indian leader. He served as a interpreter and guide for numerous expeditions, and as captain of an Indian company in the Mexican War.

Black Beaver's important role in the Civil War is illustrated in both Union and Confederate correspondence. It is truly a shame that even though Black Beaver provided such exemplary service to the military that he was never compensated for the losses he suffered when Confederate troops seized his farm and destroyed his livestock.

Black Beaver was a true friend to the army for many years, serving as an interpreter and scout during his younger days and in both the Mexican War and the Civil War: he certainly deserved better treatment by the government than he received.

REFERENCES

Civil War CD/ROM, 1996. War of the Rebellion: a compilation of the official records I the Union and Confederate armies. CD/ROM disk. Carmel, IN.: Guild Press Indiana.

Dodge, Richard Irving. 1882. Our wild Indians: thirty-three years' personal experience^ among the Red Men of the Great West. Hartford, Conn.: A. D. Worthington & Co.

Foreman, Carolyn Thomas. 1946. Black Beaver. Chronicles of Oklahoma 24:260-292,

Marcy, Randolph B. 1849. The report of Cap. R.B. Marcy's route from Fort Smith to Santa Fe. Reports of the Secretary of War, 31st Congress, 1st Session (Senate Ex. Doc 64) 169-227

Nichols, Deborah, and Lawrence Hauptman. 1997. Warriors for the Union. Civil War Times, February 1997, 35-41.

U.S. House of Representatives. 1873. Advancing the Frontier. House Report 18, 42nd Congress, 3rd Session, report to accompany bill H.R. 3371

U.S. Senate. 1909. Fremont expedition. 61st Congress, 1st session, Senate Doc. 134

Chapter 8:

Female Status and Anthropological Theory

This chapter is based on the ethnohistorical data for the Wabanaki, the Coastal Algonquians, the Shawnee, the Iroquois and the Montagnais. The ethnohistorical record Illustrates that females functioned in a variety of roles in these societies and served as Socio-political leaders, shamans, traders, midwives, ambassadors, speakers, ritual warfare Leaders and village supervisors.

The focus of this paper is on the central topic of Female status and Anthropological theory. In this paper the theoretical literature on Female status is Discussed. The topics I will address include: the Victorian Image of Females, Female Status and the Life Cycle. Male aggressiveness and dominance, missionary effects on Female status, Children's Socialization, Public Vs. Private Activity Spheres, Female Status and the World System, Fraternal Inter-Group Strength, Post-Marital Residence and Production Relations.

It is my view that Females did exert a public influence in these Northeastern Native Societies. In order to understand how and why Females exerted this influence (and thus held a position of high status within the society), a historical approach must be employed and a variety of important factors must be considered. Only within this Context can an attempt be made to understand Female status in these Northeastern Native groups.

As I have noted the question of Female status in egalitarian society is the Central concern of this paper. First, I will provide a brief summary of the anthropological Views on Female status and the historical background of these perspectives.

After presenting the more "traditional" anthropological perspective of Female status in egalitarian society, I will discuss the opposing viewpoint of several other Writers (e.g. Leacock, Grumet and Rothenberg). I believe that the theoretical perspective taken by these other writers is more accurate and that this position is supported by Cross-cultural data from the ethnographic and ethnohistorical literature from Native North America.

I also hope to illustrate that Female status in any particular society is dependent Upon a number of important factors including: economics and production relations, Socioeconomic and political complexity, fraternal inter-group strength and postmarital Residence, physiocultural dispositions acquired during socialization, missionary contact And influence, and the effects of the world system. Each of these important factors will be discussed to illustrate its relationship to Female status.

The Victorian Image and Anthropology

The theoretical perspective of Female status in egalitarian society is one that goes back to before the beginning of Anthropology as a discipline. The Victorian image of Women in non-western societies was as follows:

> "Oppressed and servile creatures, beasts of burden, chattels who could be bought or sold, eventually to be liberated by "'progress", thus attaining the enviable position of women in western society."" (E.E. Pritchard 1965:46).

This perspective laid the foundation for a very biased, ethnocentric view of Women (Divale 1976). Although anthropologists attempted to exhibit a respect for other cultures, this underlying Victorian image of Female status remained at a deeper level. At a 1955 Fawcett lecture of female students at Bedford College, E.E. Evans-Pritchard made a number of statements that illustrated his perspective on Female status in egalitarian society. Evans-Pritchard said:

> "The adult primitive woman is above all a wife, whose life is centered in her home and family ... a woman passes at marriage from under the authority of her father to that of her husband... important decisions with regard to the home, the Betrothing of daughters and sons, and so forth, rest with him alone"(E.E. Pritchard 1965:46)

Evans-Pritchard also said that "women labor(ed) only to serve men" (E.E. Pritchard 1965:46). In talking about both the primitive and the historical societies of the East and Europe he noted that they displayed a great variety of social institutions. Then he added, "but in all of them, regardless of the form of Social structure, men are always in the ascendancy, and this is perhaps more evident the higher the civilization"(E.E. Pritchard 1965:46). Later on he added, "in those Societies where any sector of the population is in a servile position, the position of women is correspondingly low with regard to the male sex"(Pritchard 1965:46). These statements by Evans-Pritchard which illustrate the "traditional" Anthropological perspective on Female status are very naive and just are not supported by the ethnohistorical evidence from Native North America.

Another problem that is clearly illustrated by the statements by Evans-Pritchard is the use of an ahistorical approach, which has been employed by many Anthropologists in their research and writing on egalitarian societies. This approach Views egalitarian societies as "static" and "unchanging". This ahistorical approach combined with the use of the concept of the "ethnographic present" has helped to greatly distort the understanding of female status in egalitarian society. As Leacock and Rosaldo & Lamphere have noted, even the "acculturation concept" suggests a static view of colonized societies and a superiority of the behaviors and institutions characteristic of the colonizer. Terms such as "traditional" and "modern" also carry an implicit value judgment with the "modern" society as superior (Leacock 1978:5) (Rosaldo & Lamphere 1974).

I would argue that an historical approach is required in order to understand the Complex factors that are involved in any study which attempts to illustrate the role of Females in egalitarian society. The fact that egalitarian societies do change and adapt to the World System is particularly clear in the ethnohistorical literature on the Iroquois and the Montagnais.

Evans-Pritchard was not the only anthropologist to support this underlying Victorian Precedent that separates Male and Female spheres and thus implying that Females never engaged in public action. Friedrich Engel's, Herbert Spencer, George Simmel and Emile Durkheim all supported this position (see Rosaldo 1980:401-409). George Simmel and Emile Durkheim expressed this viewpoint in the following account:

Up to now the sociological position of the individual woman has certain Peculiar elements. The most general of her qualities, the fact that she was a woman and as such served the functions proper to her sex, caused her to be classified with other women under one general concept. It was exactly this circumstance, which removed her from the processes of group-formation in their strict sense, as well as from actual solidarity with other women.

Because of her peculiar functions she was relegated to activities within the limits of her home, confined to devote herself to a single individual and prevented from transcending the group-relations established by marriage, family, social life, and perhaps charity and religion. (Simmel 1955:180) (Rosaldo 1980:403). ... The interests of husband and wife in marriage are... obviously opposed... It originates in the fact that the two sexes do not share equally in social life. Man is actively involved in it, while woman does little more than look on from A distance. Consequently, man is much more highly socialized than woman. (Durkheim 1951:384-385)(Rosaldo 1980:403).

Thus this perspective cast the sexes in contrastive terms with the woman and the home or domestic realm as a "given" ideology which also implied that women did not take part in public areas of a particular society. This position in not correct as the ethnohistorical evidence for some societies in Native North America shows.

All of the above anthropologist's perspectives suffer from a distinct male bias. Since the majority of ethnography has been written by male anthropologists this male bias has largely continued even today. Until recently, as I have shown, males were viewed as the dominant "public social actors" while the Females were viewed as a Peripheral group that functioned only in the private, domestic sphere. This male-biased Perspective also caused dissenting research to be either obscured or described as meaningless (Leacock 1980:4).

Due to this male-bias, the ethnographic literature on women suffers from large gaps and this is also true for Native North America. Since almost all of the early ethnographers were males, very few female activities were even mentioned in the ethnographic accounts of these anthropologists. The only female activities that were covered in these accounts concerned subjects like childcare and food preparation. Leacock has noted that this has lead "to the blanket acceptance of a universal western idea of women's status that has no empirical documentation" (Leacock 1978:247).

Female Status and the Life Cycle

A variety of ethnohistorical evidence illustrates that in many Native Cultures, Females gain increased status with age. Brown (1982:143) has noted that "women's lives appear to improve with the onset of middle age. In some societies this change is dramatic and in others moderate"

A positive change in female status is clearly related to the onset of menopause which occurs during the social age category of "middle-age". Once a woman is past her childbearing years, and the menstrual customs no longer apply to her, she receives more freedom from male authority and achieves a greater freedom of movement (Brown 1982:144) (Ezzo 1991).

Older women exert authority over kinsmen and Brown has noted that "they have the right to extract labor from them or exercise decision-making power over them"(Brown 1982:144) Older women also have a lot of influence in the marriage Arrangements in many societies, Bart has pointed out that the "institutionalization of the mother-in-law and or grandmother role tends to be associated with higher status For middle-aged women"(Bart 1969) (Brown 1982:144).

There is ample evidence in the ethnohistorical and ethnographic literature that illustrates that "as women age beyond the childbearing years, they are provided with new opportunities for achievement and recognition beyond the household" (Brown 1982:145). The anthropological literature discusses a variety of roles for older women in Native societies including: serving as midwifes (see Hayes 1975, Paul and Paul 1975), holy women (Kolenda 1978, Hungry Wolf 1980), Matchmakers (Wolf 1974), medicine women (Wright 1979a), curers (Spring 1978) and matrons (Brown 1970 and 1982). All of these positions in which middle-aged women served provided them with increased status and public influence, which went beyond the household or domestic sphere of the society.

For the Wabanki groups, Chamberlains account discussed "granddames" who were females passed "middle-age" who had the ability to speak in councils and had much more freedom from restraint (Chamberlain 1902:81; 85-86)(Morrison 1983:127). Elder females were also noted as being particularly powerful as shaman-sagamores (Levett 1983:104,105) (Eckstorn 1980).

The relationship between increased female status and age is also clear for the ethnohistorical record of the coastal Algonkian groups. In these groups, older females were recorded as serving as paramount sachems, speaking in councils, Influencing war captains, marriages and serving as shamans and traders (Smith 1907:101, Grumet 1980:49, Fox 1952:53, Beverley 1947:232, Heckewelder 1876:161, Goodard 1978:13, Simmons 1976:223, Gookin 1792:154, Williams 1866:149, Grumet 1978a and 1978b, Tantaquidgeon 1972 and Heckewelder 1876:228)

The important relationship between age and female status is also stressed by Both Zeisberger (1910:83) and Snow (1976:283) who both stated that older female shamans were thought to be very powerful among the costal Algonquian groups.

The relationship between age and increased female status is very clear for the Iroquois matrons. Indeed, the status and influence of the Iroquois females rested in the hands of the matrons or the elderly heads of households (Brown 1970). Iroquois matrons had a variety of important powers including: influencing war parties, serving as ambassadors, and determining the issues of war and peace in times of crisis (Fenton 1986:36-38). There can be no doubt that the Iroquois matrons exerted a very powerful influence in the public sphere of the League of the Iroquois.

In summary, the ethnohistorical record supplies ample evidence of a variety of roles for females in Native North America. Females achieved positions of leadership in both religious and political spheres of the society and in all of these societies, females Gained increased status once they reached "middle-age". Thus clearly the life cycle is an important factor that must be considered in any cross-cultural study of female status.

Male Aggressiveness and Dominance

Men's greater physical strength and aggressiveness have been called "universal determinants of women's status"(Quinn 1977:186). It in an established fact that males have greater physical strength than females and thus are better equipped for a more strenuous life (Quinn 1977:186)(Hutt 1972).

There is considerable debate however over what "are the differences in behavior, which result from these physiological and skeletal differences" (Quinn 1977:18). In general, it can be said that there are a number of sexual divisions of labor that are present because of these physiological and skeletal differences between the sexes.

Male participation in hunting and warfare activities in particular have been explained by anthropologists in reference to these basic biological differences between the sexes. Anthropologists have noted that hunting and warfare is a male-dominated activity because of the female requirements of childbearing, nursing, and rearing (Quinn 1977:187). Friedl has pointed out that female exclusion from warfare is also adaptive because while males can father a large number of offspring, females can bear only a few children each thus males are clearly more expendable (Quinn 1977: 187) (Friedl 1975). Another factor that has been viewed as helping to explain why males are dominant over females is the established cross-cultural finding that males are more aggressive than females (Maccoby and Jacklin 1974)(Whiting and Edwards 1973) (Quinn 1977:187,188). This greater degree of aggressiveness for males has been found to begin at age 2 and is a pattern that holds true cross-culturally for both physical and verbal aggression (Quinn 1977:188).

As Quinn has noted, "physiologically levels of aggression have been convincingly tied to levels of male hormones in both humans and subhuman primates and both males and androgenized females"(Quinn 1977:188). Other writers have viewed male aggressiveness as adaptive in defense (Voorhies 1975), species survival (Macoby and Jacklin 1973) and ambition and drive (Hutt 1972)(Quinn 1977:188).

Male aggressiveness has also been linked to the differences in socialization between boys and girls (Barry, Bacon and Child 1959) (Quinn 1977:188). These authors "show that overall sex differences in socialization is greater in those types of economy which put a premium on male strength and skill, a finding which bolsters an interpretation of male achievement motivation as a product of socialization" Quinn 1977:189)(Ember 1973).

Male aggressiveness has been used quite often as an attempt to explain why males dominate females and as Quinn has pointed out this has lead to an implicit "notion that men are somehow able to gain such rights and monopolies by aggressive use of force" (Quinn 1977:189).

Macoby and Jacklin (1974:274), who complied a review of the psychological literature on aggressiveness strongly disagrees with this view. They state:

> In adolescence and adulthood, aggression declines as the means for achieving dominance (for leadership). As the power to influence others comes to depend more and more upon competencies and mutual affection and attraction rather than simple power by assertion by force, equality of [the] sexes in power bargaining encounters becomes possible (Macoby and Jacklin 1974:274) Thus as Macoby and Jacklin point out, dominance and influence in adulthood is dependent upon a variety of personal social abilities (e.g. competence, Supportiveness, etc). The only place where males can dominate females due to their Greater physical strength and aggression is in the home (Quinn 1977:190).

One area, which as Quinn notes that has been largely overlooked by Anthropologists, is verbal aggressiveness. Verbal aggressiveness is one very important skill that greatly enhances a particular individual's ability to achieve positions of power and influence in a society. Since there are only a few studies that explore this area at all, no general cross-cultural statement can be made regarding verbal aggressiveness and the sexes(see Tiger and Spepher 1075:136) (Quinn 1977:190).

The ethnohistorical literature from Native North America, which provides evidence of females in positions of political and religious leadership clearly illustrates that while males may indeed dominant individual females in the domestic sphere due to their greater physical aggressiveness. This does not give them any distinct advantage over females in competition for positions of adult leadership in the society, which is dependent upon personal factors such as competence, supportiveness and verbal skill.

Females who obtained socio-political and religious positions of leadership in Native North America clearly had the right mixture of personal attributes in order to achieve these positions. Thus I would have to agree with Quinn's statement who sums up the importance of the greater male strength and aggressiveness by concluding that:

> Male strength and physical aggressiveness, while not plausible
> Explanations of men's collective preemption of political offices
> And authority, are plausible factors in the power of men over
> Individual women, often when these women are socially isolated And notably in the domestic context (Quinn 1977:190).

Missionary Effects on Female Status

The missionaries were an important influence on Native North American Societies, and they had an important impact on female status. Missionaries who worked with Native groups in North America had several purposes including the obvious desire to gain religious converts as well as some secondary goals of "Civilizing the Natives"(Axtell 1981)

The Iroquois and the Montagnais have the most detailed historical records that shows the changes that took place in the societies once missionary contact Began.

The Quakers worked with the Iroquois and with the help of the Seneca prophet Handsome Lake, instituted a number of important changes into Iroquois Society. As Wallace (1969:272-285) has noted, the Quakers had a model program which Handsome Lake adapted almost in its entirety (Wallace 1969:272).

The Quaker model included the introduction of farming, education, providing the Iroquois with Anglo technology, and the "Protestant ethic". Wallace summed up The Quaker "Protestant ethic" as follows:

> This ethic emphasized sobriety, marital fidelity, and observance of Contract, hard work, orderliness, a respect for equipment and Livestock, cleanliness, the duty of patiently helping back to duty Those who strayed from the path of virtue rather than killing or Otherwise retaliating upon them with violence (Wallace 1969:276) The introduction of the nuclear family by the Quakers was one of the factors That led to a decline in female status. With the introduction of the nuclear family, The ties between mothers and daughters were loosened and the maternal lineage was Greatly weakened. This change was accepted by Handsome Lake and was a key Factor in decreasing the status and power of the Iroquois matrons (Wallace 1969:284)

The Jesuits also worked with the Montagnais and they introduced a number of Important changes into Montagnais society. Just as in the Iroquois case, female status declined in Montagnais society because of the changes that the Jesuits introduced. The Jesuits introduced premarital chastity, male courtship, monogamy, marital fidelity, Education, the nuclear family and patrilocality. The introduction of the nuclear Family and patrilocality as well as other changes resulted in the loss of some Independence and decreased status for Montagnais females (Leacock 1980)

Quite obviously missionary contact brings about numerous changes in any Native society that they come into contact with. Clearly missionaries were merely the front guard of the advancing world System that came into contact with Native North American Indian societies and they must be included in any cross-cultural study of female status because of the rapid social change that took place under their influence.

For both the Iroquois and the Montagnais females the end result of missionary contact was a vast decrease in status and a great decline in their ability to have Influence in the public sphere of these two societies.

CHILDREN'S SOCIALIZATION

Females have the primary responsibility of socializing their children. Chodorow has pointed out that this accounts for vast differences between male and female personalities. The basic difference between a girl's socialization process and a boy's is that a girl is able to achieve her proper gender identity by simply modeling her mother, while a boy must eventually replace his identification with his mother to an identification with his father or other adult males in the society (Quinn 1977:193)(Chodorow 1974). Chodorow has argued that unlike mothers who are in almost constant reach of their children, a father is often quite inaccessible to his son because in most societies males do not play a primary role in taking care of the children and adult males are involved in activities that keep them away from home much of the time (e.g. hunting, warfare, and trading). Chodorow notes as follows:

> As a result, a boy's gender identification often becomes a "Positional" identification, with aspects of his father's clearly Or not so clearly defined male role, rather than a more generalized "personal" identification- a diffuse identification with his father's personality, values and behavioral traits- that could grow out of A real relationship to his father (Chodorow 1974:49).

Thus a boy must deny attachment and dependence upon his mother and devalue femininity in order to achieve his proper gender identification while a girl achieves her gender identity through a continuous, affective relationship with her mother (Quinn 1977:194).

Bacon and Child (1959) have noted that a boy's training is oriented toward achievement and independence while a girl's training is oriented toward nurturance and responsibility (Quinn 1977:194). A boy's training is also delayed and involves a "transitional period of universalistic membership in a group of peers rather than particularistic role relations"(Quinn 1977:194)

Women's particular interactions tend to be cross-generational and it includes a variety of relationships and responsibilities while men's interactions tend to be restricted to one generation, cross-cut kinship units and tend to involve more specific relationships and responsibilities (Quinn 1977:194) (Ross 1981,1983,1986).

Rosaldo (1974) has pointed out that this significant difference in socialization between the sexes has a very important effect on individual status. She points out that since boys interaction spheres involve competitive peer groups a boy achieves status that is associated with formal roles and authority. A girl however interacts with people as individuals and thus she is socialized to achieve her interests by making appeals to other people and being nurturant, responsive and kind (Quinn 1977:194). This difference in socialization results in males competing for status and helps to explain why men continue to enjoy an advantage over females in the public sphere and why females are often kept in the domestic sphere of society (Quinn 1977:194). Quinn notes:

> Politically, this means that men occupy, and women are excluded from, the ranked, institutionalized positions. In economic terms, it means that women's work is relatively less public, and done individually or in small loosely organized groups. The products of this work are used within the family and household, or, if distributed more widely, appropriated by men in their pursuit of prestige. The more marked the differentiation between domestic and public spheres of activity in a given society, the more women's political and economic status will suffer (Quinn 1974:194).

Although some studies have attempted to link task socialization with sexual dependency (see Chodorow 1974; and Whiting & Edwards 1973) Macoby & Joacklin 1974 have concluded "there is no consistent tendency across relevant studies for girls to be more dependent, as might be expected from Chodorow's(1974:11) suggestion that boy's sex-role learning involves denial of attachment or relationship, particularly of what the boy takes to be dependence or need for another, while girls continue to be dependent on their mothers in adulthood"(Chodorow 1974:1 l)(quoted from Quinn 1977: 196). Thus, as Quinn has noted "Whether the sex difference in dependency is innate, or whether it is due to the particular socialization experience by Chodorow, remains unresolved" (Quinn 1977:197).

Public and Private Activity Spheres

Levi-Strauss' theoretical position assumes that women occupy a position of inferiority to males. Levi-Strauss' significant impact on symbolic anthropology has led to the development of a male/female dichotomy. This dichotomy associates men with culture and public spheres of activity while the female position is associated with Nature and private spheres of activity (see Leacock 1978; Ortner 1974). This dichotomy thus implies that females did not have any influence in public spheres of activity and thus are therefore inferior to males.

There are a number of explanations that have been put forth by Anthropologists to attempt to explain how this private/public dichotomy developed. Harris(1977) And Divale & Harris(1976) have speculated that the combination of scare resources, the dangers of overpopulation and warfare made female fertility a threat and thus lead to Male dominance in early human societies (Leacock 1978:3).

Mullassaux (1975) believes that although sexual equality is present in hunting and gathering societies, women become inferior to males in horticultural societies Because of the value of their reproductive capacity.(Leacock 1978:3). Friedl also believes that females are inferior to males because of their childbearing function (see Friedl 1978, Leacock 1980:3).

Another key factor in the evolution of a public/private dichotomy is trade, which lead to the development of ranking in Native societies and laid the foundation for "Inequalities both among women and men and between women and men"(Leacock 1978:13) (see also Trigger 1960 and 1962a).

Collier (1974) has written an important article that discusses the role of females in politics and their activities in the public sphere. She noted that both "natives and Ethnographers tend to view politics as a male pastime"(Collier 1974:89). She also pointed out that female participation in politics is patterned but as anthropologists often have a hard time discovering Native models of social structure because the Natives themselves usually do not discuss the role of females in political affairs (Collier 1974:89).

Collier follows Barths (1966) theoretical position, which focuses on a system of constraints and incentives that channel individual choices. I shall discuss Collier's article in more detail in the section on inter-group strength and post-marital residence because the more specific focus of her article discuses descent systems and Post-marital residence and how this effects female status.. Her more general thesis however is most important for the present discussion. She believes that women must be viewed as "social actors whose efforts to control the social environment are channeled by cultural rules, by available resources, and by the choices of others within the social System"(Collier 1974:90). Sanday (1974) has written an article, which focuses on female status in the public domain. In her cross-cultural study she noted that females had achieved a relatively high status in the public domain in a number of societies (Sanday 1974:190). Sanday uses four dimensions for coding female status in the public sphere. These dimensions are: female material control (over resources), the demand for female produce (either internal or external), female political participation (the ability to influence public policy) and the existence of female solidarity groups (Sanday 1974:192).

Sanday believes that in many societies males have been in a more advantageous position to gain control over strategic resources because males devoted their primary energies to defense and subsistence while women devoted their primary energies to reproduction. This enabled males to gain control over strategic resources and resulted in a position of inferiority for many females (Sanday 1974:205).

Sanday also noted that the primary factors that influence the balance of power between the sexes include: male absence, ecological factors and the demand for female goods. As I have already pointed out, both female participation in subsistence and the demand for female goods has had a positive effect on female status. Sanday has also pointed out that female political and economic power is legitimized by the societal cultural system. One good example of this from Native North America is the Shawnee, who have an important female deity (see Voegelin & Voegelin 1944).

Female Status and the World System

There can be little doubt that female status has been influenced by the world economic system. Leacock has noted that all of the societies that have been studied by anthropologists have been influenced by a "world socio-political systems which oppress women"(Leacock 1978:247). Anthropologists have only recently admitted (within the past three decades) to the existence of a world political system and have only begun to study the influence and changes it has brought to the egalitarian societies it came into contact with (see Wallerstein 1974; Sacks 1976; Saffiote 1978 and Sanday 1973).

One of the key elements of the world system was the development of trade, which is another important variable, which must be understood in order to understand female Status in egalitarian society and how it changed due to culture contact with the advancing World system. The introduction of trade goods into Native North America had several important effects. European trade goods lead to fierce competition between groups. Native groups also became dependent upon European trade goods for their very existence. This lead to the development of ranking in Native societies which then laid the foundation for as Leacock has noted for "inequalities both among women and men and between women and men"(Leacock 1980:13)(see also Trigger 1960 and 1962a).

With the development of ranking in Native North American societies, the "public Vs private" dichotomy that I have already discussed began to develop. The public sector of the economy was concerned with surplus production and trade, while the private sector of the economy involved sub-sistence production for the household (Sanday 1974). Although women that were involved in trade and production for the market retained a very high status in the public sphere (for example Seneca Iroquois females), the male roles of hunting and warfare usually resulted in males controlling trade and having the responsibility for external political relations. All of these developments lead to the increased importance of patrilineal lines and the decrease of female status and influence (Leacock 1978:14)(Ember and Ember 1973; Engels 1972).

North American Native societies were also greatly influenced and changed By the effects of colonization and capitalism as Leacock has noted

> "The economic trust of colonization, sometimes masked by ide-ology, sometimes overt and undisguised, was always present, but the relationship between economic exploitation of colo-nized peoples and the development of capitalism as a world sys-tem emerged most clearly in the late nineteenth and twentieth centuries. Together and separately, the case studies show how the transformation of production relations worked as a whole. The crucial mechanisms were production for commodity exchange and reliance on commodities (Leacock 1981:19).

Since the colonizers presented both the demands and their technology to the males, the men had greater access to cash. This lead to the "eco-nomic dependency of women and, as a result, the emergence of the patri-archal nuclear family"(Leacock 1981:19).

Kathryn Ward has pointed out that a number of studies have shown that female status declines as a result of economic development and con-tact with the world system (see also Boserup 1970; United Nations 1980). She noted that during the process of economic development "women's tra-ditional sources of livelihood are disrupted and without a sex-equitable redistribution of the new economic and social resources generated by eco-nomic growth (Ward 1984: l)(see also Papanek 1976; Tinker 1976). Ward also notes that most researches have ignored two important social conse-quences of contact with the world system: a decline in female status and high levels of fertility. Ward's central hypothesis is as follows:

> The major hypothesis I advance in this book is that the intrusion of the world-system through foreign investment from and trade

dependency on core nations has operated to reduce women's status relative to men's. Under development and the export to developing Countries of Western definitions of women's proper place have produced a double burden for women in developing nations. Men and the TNCs often define women's proper roles as reproducers and unpaid subsistence laborers within the domestic sphere. As a consequence, women experience not only the material consequences of underdevelopment and the disruption of their traditional sources of economic livelihood, but also limited access to the new mode of monetary or wage labor production introduced by the world-system (Ward 1984:3).

Ward also makes two other key statements, both of which are true for Native North American societies. The first, is that when new agricultural technology is introduced into a region, the males are usually the only ones who have access to the new techniques, crops and credit "despite the fact that the females have typically been the primary agricultural producers"(Ward 1984:3)(see also Boserup 1970; Tinker 1976; And United Nations 1980).

The second statement is that because of the influence of the world system, female traders are relegated to local trade routes in almost all cases while the males control national and international trade (Ward 1984:3)(see also Mintz 1971). The historical record illustrates these changes most clearly in the case studies of the Montagnais and the Iroquois. Thus, as Native societies became dependent upon the United States (in large measure due to the fur trade), female status in these groups declined because their traditional economic functions were disrupted (like agriculture and trade). Eleanor Leacock has written several papers that discuss the impact of the world system on the Montagnais society. I have already discussed the specific changes that took place in Montagnais society under the influence of the Jesuit missionary program. Another fine example of the impact of the world system is the case study of the Iroquois that I presented and how contact with the Quakers changed Iroquois Society. Leacock stresses the same facts that Ward does in noting that as Native groups came into contact with the world system; females lost their economic resource base and the colonizers always addressed their demands and innovations to the males (Leacock 1980:19)

Another thing that Leacock points out is that female status declined in part, because the ideology of colonialism is male dominance. She also warned against using an ahistorical approach which projects the current conditions of today into History.

"Furthermore, to project the conditions of today's world onto the totality, of human history, and to consider women's oppression as inevitable, affords an important ideological buttress for those in power. Arguments about universal female subordination gloss over the structure of women's oppression in capitalist society and the negative and persisting effects of colonialism and imperialism on women's status." "The idea of women's autonomy is then presented as a Western ideal, foreign to the cultural heritages of Third World peoples. The fact, however, is that women retained great autonomy in much of the precolonial world, and relegated to each other and to men through public as well as private procedures, as they carried out their economic and social responsibilities and protected their rights. Female and male Societies of various kinds operated reciprocally within larger kin and community contexts, before the principal of male dominance with the individual families was taught by missionaries, defined by legal statutes, and solidified by the economic relations of colonialism, in fact, as women anthropologists' focus of women's activities in societies around the world, they are finding many attitudes and practices that indicate women's former status and persisting importance"(Leacock 1980:315)(see also Lebef 1963)(Reiter 1975).

Thus, the impact of the world system on Native North American groups is an important variable that must be considered in any cross-cultural study of female status. The evidence clearly shows that female status declined due to the impact of the world system.

Fraternal Inter-Group Strength and Post-Marital Residence

Fraternal inter-group strength and post-marital residence rules are also important factors that effect female status (Ember 1974), Collier has noted that females in patrilocal societies must attempt to exert influence through her husband or son. Thus females worked to promote the interest of her husband or son in the patrilocal domestic group, which puts them into conflict with males, who work to bond lineages together (Collier 1974:92).

Another important point that Collier has noted is that female domestic quarrels do indeed effect the wider political alignments of a group. This is a fact that many anthropologists have ignored (Collier 1974:92). Instead of stressing the compliance of a female that must marry into a patrilocal extended household, Collier stresses that the female can look forward to having sons since the amount of influence she will have in The society will be based, at least in part, on the status that her son will achieve. Collier follows a position similar to Barths in viewing females as important social actors in Society, working to maximize their influence. Collier notes that the "ambitious woman will use all her political knowledge to increase her sons inheritance and all her feminine wiles to persuade her husband to set up a separate household where she may have more Control over family resources"(Collier 1974:93).

In discussing the social importance of domestic quarrels, Collier points out that women's quarrels provide a forum for focusing attention on critical issues. Since issue recognition is the first step in the process of political decision-making, this fact should not be overlooked (Collier 1974:94; Clark 1968). Thus even in societies where women may not speak in councils, they can as Collier notes "affect decisions by causing an uproar that forces others to pay attention to their wishes"(Collier 1974:94).

Collier also stresses that females play an important part in the process of social change and that as "new resources enter a political field, both men and women seek advantage from expanded opportunities, and the course of change necessarily reflects the complex interplay of male and female tactics"(Collier 1974:96). Good examples of female tactics that were employed to respond to new resources (for example trade), were discussed for the Algonquians, Iroquois and Montagnais. Thus, Collier's general, cross-cultural theoretical statements on females as social actors is backed up by the evidence from Native North America.

Louise Lamphere, in her article titled "Women in Domestic Groups" also takes the same theoretical perspective as Collier did in her article. She also stressed the female relationship to power and authority changes as she ages and her children become adults, and so the developmental cycle (that I have already discussed) is an important part of her argument (Lamphere 1974:99). She also views females as social actors who employ particular strategies to obtain desired ends, "whether this entails making decisions themselves, exercising influence over those who make decisions, or circumventing the domestic power structure"(Lamphere 1974:99). Lamphere concludes as follows:

> "Women quarrel with or dominate other women when it is in their Interest to do so; they share and exchange with other women when it suits their own goals. Cooperation and conflict among women in Families or kin groups cannot be understood

without reference to domestic power structure, to women's
place within it, and to the factors that shape the relationship
between the family and the larger society"(Lamphere
1974:112).

Other important factors that effect female status include polygamy,
and descent and post-marital residence patterns. Some writers have stated
that polygamy reduces the Domestic power a wife will have over her husband while others have stressed that if Men are very desirous of being
polygamists it can actually have a positive effect on female status (Quinn
1977:211; Netting 1969). In any case, since only the Montagnais and the
Western Abenaki practiced polygamy historically, and even among these
groups it was a relatively rare practice, for the purposes of the groups discussed in this paper, polygny is clearly not an important factor.

A number of anthropologists have noted that descent is an important
factor in female status (see Martin 1975; Friedl 1975; Schelegel 1972 and
Brown 1970). The fact that the Iroquois and the Delaware both had matrilineal descent systems and matrilocal post-marital residence patterns is one
of the factors that had a positive influence on female status in these groups.

Martin has noted that in horticultural, matrilineal societies, female
status is almost universally high (from Quinn 1977:211). Martin uses the
Iroquois as an example and stated that since females are the focus of the
social structure and females also control resource allocations they "therefore wielded considerable decision-making influence"(from Quinn
1977:211; see also Richards 1957).

Matrilocal residence is also an important factor in female status.
Friedl has noted that females in matrilineal and matrilocal societies have a
greater opportunity to achieve domestic equality (Quinn 1977:213). Martin has stressed that matrilocal residence patterns have extradomestic
implications noting that the power or status of Iroquoian females depended
not only on their control of production of resources but also because
"related women remained together throughout life, forming tightly knit
residential as well as social units"(from Quinn 1977:213). Thus Martin
emphasizes the formation of fraternal inter-groups, which strengthened
female status. He also notes that matrilocality disperses related males at the
same time; it allows for the formation of domestic coalitions among
females (Quinn 1977:214). Thus for the matrilocal Iroquois and Delaware,
female status was clearly influenced positively by the ability of females in
these societies to act in groups and thus as Quinn notes to gain "both
domestic control and extra domestic influence over Men"(Quinn
1977:214). Thus, clearly matrilineal descent and matrilocal post-marital

residence are two factors that must be considered in any cross-cultural study of female status.

Production Relations

Another key variable in the understanding of the status of females in egalitarian society is production relations. It is very important to note that in egalitarian societies, there is an equal participation of all adults in the economy. In these societies, decisions are made by the group and authority is dispersed. Leacock noted:

> "All manner of social arts are used by both men and women to Influence people, resolve problems, and hold groups together. These range from endless talk and discussion through myth making, song, dance and ritual to merciless teasing, disapproval and threat of social isolation"(Leacock 1978:9,10).

One good example of a society like this that I have already discussed at some length is the Montagnais. Also as I have already noted, Iroquoian females had control over the production and distribution of agricultural resources. This control over the economic resources of the society was one of the factors that enabled Iroquois females to have such high status and public influence in the society (Brown 1970:235) Jeneness summed it up well:

> If women among the Iroquois enjoyed more privileges and possessed Greater freedom than the women of other tribes, this was due. .. To the important place that agriculture held in their economic life, And the distribution of labor.. .[which left] the entire cultivation Of the fields and the acquisition of the greater part of the food Supply to the women"(Jenness 1932:137)(Brown 1970:235)

Thus the Iroquois females were able to influence male activities such as warfare and hunting because they controlled the essential provisions for these male Activities (Leacock 1978:253).

Sacks article reexamines Engles' ideas on the social position of females relative to males. Engels uses a materialist approach and he thought that Female's position (or status) in a particular group varied as he stated "according to the prevailing economic and political relationships of the society (Sacks 2975:211).

In Engels "Origin of the Family, Private Property, and the State", 1891 he discusses the rise of private property and how it worked to undermine egalitarian societies and thus cause a decline in female status. His study contrasts the difference between class and nonclass societies (see Sacks 1975:212).

In reexamming Engles work, Sacks comes to several conclusions. She focuses on public labor, the family and private property and shows how each of these variables affected female status. She also redefined Engels' terminology and adds a modification by stating that in her view females either function as social actors or wifely dependents. Her major difference from Engels is that, in her view, private property did not lead directly to lower status for women. She thinks that "class societies have used the family to circumscribe and subordinate women"(Sacks 1975:213) I have illustrated this point in several places in this paper when I discussed how the missionaries worked to make the nuclear family the norm among the Montagnais and the Iroquois.

Sacks central point it that while property ownership is an important variable for female status, it is even more important that females as she states "have adult status in the social sphere"(Sacks 1975:234). She also points out that with the development of use and exchange value a dichotomy was made between the family and the larger society (Sacks 1975:234). She sums it up as follows:

> But the dichotomization of family and society, which is especially strong in class societies, makes women responsible for the production of private use value and makes men responsible for the production of exchange values. The distinction between production for use and production for exchange places a heavy responsibility on women to maintain themselves as well as exchange workers and to rear future exchange and maintenance workers. In this context, wage work (or social labor) becomes an additional burden and in no way changes women's responsibility for domestic work. For full social equality, men's and women's work must be of the same kind; the production of social use values. For this to happen, family and society cannot remain separate economic spheres of life. Production, consumption, child-rearing, and economic decision-making all need to take place in a single social sphere-something analogous to the Iroquois gens as described by Engels, or the production brigades of China during the Great Leap Forward. What is now private family work must become public work for women to become fully social adults"(Sacks 1975:234).

One good example of this that I have provided in this paper is to contrast the Iroquois and the Montagnais. In the Iroquois case, Seneca females remained important as traders and thus they had exchange value in the public sphere. In the Montagnais case, females were not important as traders and the males only functioned as traders, thus in Montagnais society male work became associated with exchange value while female work began to have only use value. The result of this difference was that while Seneca females retained their high status in the society, Montagnais female status began to decline.

Both Sanday (1975) and Friedl (1975:8,9) have noted that contribution to production is a necessary but not a sufficient condition for the improvement of women's status (Quinn 1977:203). Another factor that must be considered is male absence and warfare since both of these factors are closely tied to production relations.

Sanday (1975) has noted that when the requirement for defense is strong, males move out of the subsistence sphere and into the defense sphere. Under conditions of long periods of warfare females actually displace males in subsistence activities thus "leading to a balanced division of labor and women's high public status" (quoted from Quinn 1977:203). The best example of this is the Iroquois.

Iroquois males were away from the village for extended periods of time in fighting, hunting, trading or on diplomatic missions. Wallace has noted that "the Iroquois population was, in effect, divided into two parts: sedentary females and nomadic males"(Wallace 1971:369). Thus female status was strengthened in Iroquois society because of the prolonged absence of the males.

Thus the important factors that must be considered under production relations include female labor, male absence and female trade. All of these factors help to increase female independence and status within a particular society. As Quinn(1977) has noted:

"The indispensability of female labor, the unavailability of male labor due to male absence, and the economic independence of women through trade may combine to explain cases in which women control their own production and set the stage for their political participation as well"(Quinn 1977:205).

In summary, the factors that I have discussed in relation to production relations seems to be most applicable to the Coastal Algonquians, Iroquois and the Montagnais societies. Trade was an important factor in both the Coastal Algonquian and Iroquois groups. Females played an important economic role in these societies by serving as traders and this role helped them to retain more independence and thus in creased female status in both of these societies. Female control over production resources was an important factor for the Iroquois and the Montagnais and this was one of the factors, which clearly helped to support female status in both of these groups. In view of all of this evidence I think that any cross-cultural study of female status must consider production relations as an important variable that either adds to or subtracts from female status in a particular society.

Conclusion

In conclusion, I will like to sum up the major points that I have presented in this paper. In this paper I have discussed the theoretical literature on female status. The topics that I have addressed include: the Victorian Image of Females, female status and the life cycle, male aggressiveness and dominance, missionary effects on female status, children's socialization, public vs. private activity spheres, female status and the world system, fraternal inter-group strength and post-marital residence and production relations.

I strongly disagree with the position taken by a number of writers including: E.E. Pritchard (1965), Friedrich Engles (1972), Herbert Spencer, George Simmel (1955), Emile Durkheim (1951) and Alfred Miller (1968) that females in Native societies were only important within the domestic sphere of a particular society and thus held no individual or collective public power. This position is still accepted by some writers today and is still found in some of the secondary source material on Native North America.

The ethnohistorical evidence that I have discussed in this paper clearly illustrates that females functioned in a wide variety of roles as social actors in the public sphere of these Native groups. Females in these Northeastern groups served as: political leaders, shamans, ritual warfare leaders, village supervisors, council speakers and traders. I strongly agree with the position taken by several writers including Leacock, Rothenberg and Grumet who each stress that females did not function only in the domestic sphere in Native societies but were indeed important social actors in the public sphere. The historical evidence that I have presented for each of these groups supports this position.

I think that through the use of ethnohistorical methods, and a variety of primary source materials, a much more accurate picture of how females functioned historically in particular Native groups can be constructed. Before an accurate picture of how these Native groups functioned historically can be constructed, the roles of Females in these groups must be discovered. The "traditional" notion that females were important only in the domestic sphere of a society is clearly rejected by the evidence that I have cited from the historical literature. Thus by documenting the variety of roles that females did have in Native North America, the first step in achieving a more accurate picture of how these Native groups functioned historically can be achieved.

I also believe that research on female status is a good laboratory that can allow the anthropologist to study the process of historical change in Native groups. By doing comparative research that focuses on how female status changed as a result of contact with the world system, a better understanding of how the social structure adapted to these changes can be discovered.

It is also true, as Katherin Weist (1982:46) has pointed out, that the treatment of Indian women was a major factor for the designation of the term "savage". By using historical methods to study primary source accounts, a more accurate picture of the roles of females in Native groups can be achieved. Alfred Miller stated that "nothing so strikingly distinguishes civilized from savage life as the treatment of women. It is in every particular in favor of the former"(Miller 1968:70). This is a viewpoint that is incorrect in view of the ethnohistorical evidence that I have presented in this paper that clearly shows that female status declined as a result of contact with "civilization".

In summary, I believe that there is still much more work that needs to be done on this topic. The cross-cultural study of female status is merely the first step that is required in order to achieve a more accurate historical picture of how these Native Northeastern groups functioned. As Valerie Mathers has noted "the historical surface has been barely scratched on the subject of Indian women" (Mathers 1975:137).

REFERENCES

Axtell, James, editor
1981 The Indian Peoples of Eastern America: A Documentary History of The Sexes. New York: Oxford University Press.

Barry, H. Child. I.L., Bacon, M.K.
1959 "Relation of child training to subsistence economy.". American Anthropologist 61:5163.

Bart, Pauline
1969 "Why women's status changes in middle age. The turns of the Social ferris wheel". Sociological Symposium 3:1-18.

Barth, Frederick
1966 "Models of Social Organization". Royal Anthropological Institute Occasional Papers #23.

Beverly, Robert
1947 (orig 1705). "The History and Present State of Virginia", Louis Wright editor. Chapel Hill: The University of North Carolina Press.

Boserup, E.
1970 "Women's Role in Economic Development". New York: St. Martin's Press.

Brown, Judith K.
1971 "Economic Organization and the position of women among theIroquois". Ethnohistory 17:151-167.

1982 "Cross-cultural Perspectives on Middle-aged Women". Current Anthropology 23:143-153.

Chamberlain, Montague
1902 "The Primitive Life of the Wapanaki Women". Acadiensis 2(2): 75-86.

Chodorow, N.
1974 "Family structure and feminine personality". In: Women, Culture, And Society. Rosaldo, M.Z. and Lamphere, L, eds. Stanford: Stanford University Press.

Clignet, R.
1970 "Many wives. Many Powers: Authority and Power in Polygnous Families". Evanston: Northwestern University Press.

Clark, Terry N.
  1967 "The Concept of Power", In T. Clark, editor. Community Structure & Decision Making, Comparative Analyses, San Francisco.

Collier, J.F.
  1974 "Women in Politics", In: Woman, Culture and Society. Rosaldo,
  M.Z. and Lamphere, L, eds. Stanford: Stanford University Press,
  Pp. 89-96.

Divale, William Tulio
  1975 "Female Status and Cultural Evolution: A Study in Ethnogra-
  pher Bias", Behavior Science Research 11:169-211.

Divale, William T and Marvin Harris
  1976 "Population, Warfare and the Male Supremacist Complex",
  American Anthropologist 78: 521-38.

Durkheim, Emile.
  1951 "Suicide"(Glencoe, 111: Free Press), pp. 384-85.

Eckstorm, Fannie Hardy
  1980 "Old John Neptune and Other Maine Indian Shamans" [1945]
  Orono, Maine: The University Of Maine Press.

Ember, C.A.
  1972 "The effect of feminine task assignment on the social behavior
  of boys", Ethos 1:424-39.

Ember, Carol and Melvin
  1973 "The conditions Favoring Matrilocal Vs. PatrilocaJ Residence".
  American Anthropologist 73:571-594.

Ember, Carol
  1974 "An Evolution of Alternative Theories of Matrilocal Versus
  Patrilocal Residence" Behavior Science Research Journal 9:2.

Engels, Friedrich
  1971 "The Origin of the Family, Private Property, and the State" New
  York: International Publishers.

Evans-Pritchard
  1965 "The Position of Women in Primitive Societies and in our
  Own". In E.E. Evans-Prithcard:, The Position of Women In Primitive
  Societies and Other Essays in Social Anthropology. London: Faber
  and Faber.

Ezzo, David A.
1991 "Female Status and the Life Cycle", Pp. 137-144 in:
Papers of the Twenty-Second Algonquian Conference, William
Cowan, editor Ottawa: Carleton University.

Fenton, William
1986 "Leadership in the Northeastern Woodlands of North America".
American Indian Quarterly, Winter 1986: Pp. 21-44.

Fox, George
1952 "Journals of George Fox", John L. Nickalls, editor. London:
Cambridge University Press.

Friedl, E.
1975 "Women and Men: an Anthropologist's View" New York:
Hold, Rinehart and Winston.

Goddard, Ives.
1977 "Delaware", In: Handbook of North American Indians, Vol. 15,
Northeast, William C. Sturtevant and Bruce G. Trigger, eds, pp. 213-
239. Washington: Smithsonian Institution.

Gookin, Daniel
1792(orig. 1674) "Historical Collections of the Indians of New England" Collections of the Massachusetts Historical Society, 1st series,
Vol 1, pp. 141-229.

Grumet, Robert Steven
1978a "We are not so Great Fools", Changes in Upper Delawarn
Socio-Political Life, 1630-1758". Ph.D. dissertation, Anthropology
Department, Rutgers University.

1978b "An Analysis of Upper Delawarn Land Sales in Northern New
Jersey". In: Papers of the 9th Algonquian Conference, William
Cowan, ed. Pp. 23-35, Ottawa: Carleton University Press.

1980   "Sunskquaws, Shamans, and Tradeswomen: Middle Atlantic
Coastal Algonkian Women During the 17th and 18th Centuries" In
Women and Colonization: Anthropological Perspectives. Mona Eti-
enne and Eleanor Leacock, eds. Pp 43-62. New York.: Praeger.

Harris, Marvin
1978 "Why Men Dominate Women". The New York Times
Magazine, November 13, pg/ 46.

Hayes, Rose Oldfied.
1976 "Female genital mutilation, fertility control, women's roles, and The patrilineage in modern Sudan". A functional analysis. American Ethnologist 2:617-33.

Heckewelder, John
1817 "History, Manners and Customs of the Indian Nations" Philadelphia: Historical Society of Pennsylvania.

Hungry Wolf, Beverly
1979 "The Ways of My Grandmothers". New York: Morrow.

Hutt, C.
1972 "Males and Females". Baltimore: Penquin.

Jeness, Diamond
1932 "The Indians of Canada", Bulletin of the National Museum of Canada, no. 65, Ottawa, F.A. Acland, Printer to the King.

Kolenda, Pauline
1977 "Caste in contemporary India: Beyond organic solidarity" Reading, Mass. Benjamin/Cummings.

Lamphere, Louise
1973 "Strategies, Cooperation and Conflict Among Women in Domestic Groups" In: Woman, Culture and Society, Michelle Zimbalist Rosaldo and Louise Lamphere, eds, pp. 97-112.

Leacock, Eleanor
1958 "Status among the Montagnais-Naskapi of Labrador" Ethnohistory 5(3): Pp. 200-209.

1978 "Women's Status in Egalitarian Society: Implications for Social Evolution"., Current Anthropology 19, 2:247-75.

1980a "Montagnais Women and the Jesuit Program for Colonization" In: Women and Colonization: Anthropological Perspectives, Mona Etienne and Eleanor Leacock, eds, Pp, 25-42. New York: Praeger.

1981 "Women, Development, and Anthropological Facts and Fiction: In: Myths of Male Dominance, edited by Eleanor Leacock.

1982 "The Montagnais-Naskapi". In: Myths of Male Dominance edited by Eleanor Leacock.

1983 Seveneenth Century Montagnais Social Relations and Values" In: Handbook of North American Indians, Vol 15 Subarctic. William C. Sturtevant and June Helm, eds. Pp. 190-195, Washington: Smithsonian Institution.

1981 "Ethnohistorical Investigation of Egalitarian Politics in Eastern North America, In: The Development of Political Organization In Native North America. Elisabeth Tooker, editor. From the 1979 Proceedings of the American Ethnological Society, Pp. 17-31.

Lebeuf, Annie, M.D.
1963 "The role of Women in the political organization of African Societies" in Women of Tropical Africa, Denise Paulme, ed. London: Routledge & Kegan Paul.

Levett, Christopher
1628 A Voyage into New England Begun in 1623 and Ended in 1624. Pp 79-139. In: Christopher Levett of York, The Pioneer Colonist In Casco Bay, James P. Baxter, editor, 1893. Portland Maine: The Gorges Society.

Maccoby, E.E. Jacklin, C.N.
1974 "The Psychology of Sex Differences. Stanford: Stanford University Press.

Martin, M.K, Voorhies, B.
1975 "Female of the Species". New York: Columbia University Press.

Mathers, Valerie S.
1976 "A New Look at the Role of Women in Indian Society" American Indian Quarterly, 2:131-139.

Meillassoux, Claude
1975 "Femmes, grenier, et capitaux. Paris: Masspero.

Miller, Afred J.
1968 "The West of Alfred Jacob Miller from the Notes and Water Colors in the Walters Art Gallery with an Account of the Artist by Marvin C. Ross", Norman: University of Oklahoma Press.

Mintz, S.
    1971 "Men, women and trade" Comparative Studies in Society and History, 13:47-69.

Morrison, Alvin H.
    1983 "Wabanaki Women Extraordinaire: A Sampler From Fact and Fancy" Pp. 125-136 In: Papers of the 14th Algonquian Conference. William Cowan, editor. Ottawa: Carleton University.

Netting, R. Me.
    1969 "Women's weapons: the politics of domesticity among the Kofyar", American Anthropologist 71:37-45.

Ortner, Sherry B.
    1974 "Is Female to Male as Nature is to Culture" In: Michelle Zimbalist Rosaldo and Louise Lamphere, eds. Woman, Culture, and Society. Stanford: Stanford University Press.

Papanek, H.
    1975 "Women in Cities: Problems and Perspectives" In: Women and World Development, edited by I. Tinker and M. Bramsen. Washington D.C. Overseas Development Council, pp. 54-69.

Paul, Louis and Benjamin Paul
    1976 "The Maya midwife as a sacred specialist. A Guatemalan Case" American Ethnologist 2:707-26.

Quinn, Noami
    1977 "Anthropological Studies on Women's Status" In: Annual Review of Anthropology, 1977 6:181-225.

Reiter, R.B.
    1976 "Toward an Anthropology of Women", New York: Monthly Review Press.

Richards, Cara B.
    1957 "Martiarchy or Mistake: The role of Iroquois Women through time", Proceedings of the 1957 Annual Spring Meeting of the American Ethnological Society, Pp. 36-45.

Rosaldo, Michelle Zimbalist and Louise Lamphere editors.
    1974 "Women, Culture and Society". Stanford: Stanford University Press.

Rosaldo, Michelle Zimbalist
    1980 The Use and Abuse of Anthropology: Reflections on Feminism And Cross-Cultural Understanding. Signs 5:389-417.

Ross, Marc, Howard
1981 "Socioeconomic Complexity, Socialization, and Political Dif-
ferentiation: A Cross-Cultural Study".

1982 "Political Decision Making and Conflict: Additional Cross-Cultural Codes and Scales, Ethnology 22:169-192.

1986 "Female Political Participation: A Cross-Cultural Explanation",
American Anthropologist, 88: Pp. 843-858.

Sacks, Karen
1975 "Engels Revisited: Women, The Organization of Production
and Private Property", In Toward an Anthropology of Women,
Edited by Rayna R. Reiter. New York: Monthy Review.

Saffiote, Heleeth
1977 "Women in Class Society", New York: Monthly Review Press.

Sanday, Peggy H.
1973 "Toward a Theory of the Status of Women", American
Anthropologist 75:1682-1700.

1974 "Female Status in the Public Domain", In: Women, Culture
And Society, edited by Michelle Zimbalist Rosaldo and Louise
Lamphere, Stanford: Stanford University Press.

Schlegel, A.
1972 "Male Dominance and Female Autonomy: Domestic Authority
In Matrilineal Societies. New Haven: Human Relations Area
Files Press.

Simmel, George
1955 "Conflict and the Web of Group Affiliations", New York:
Macmillan Publishing Company, p. 180.

Simmons, William S.
1975 "Southern New England Shamanism: An Ethnographic
Reconstruction", In : Papers of the 7th Algonquian Conference,
Edited by William Cowan, Ottawa: Carleton University Press,
Pp. 217-256.

Smith, John.
1907 "The General Historie of Virginia, New England and the Summer Isles, 2 vols, Glasgow: James Maclehose and Sons.

Snow, Dean
    1976 "The Solon Petroglyphs and Eastern Abanaki Shamanism",
    In: Papers of the Seventh Algonquian Conference, William
    Cowan, editor. Ottawa: Carleton University Press.

Spring, Anita
    1977 "Epidemiology of spirit possession among the Luvale of
    Zambia" In: Women in ritual and symbolic roles, edited By Judith
    Hoch-Smith and Anita Spring, New York:Plenum, Pp. 165-190.

Tantaquidgeon, Gladys
    1973 "Folk Medicine of the Delaware and Related Algonkian
    Indians, Pennsylvania Historical and Museum Commission
    Anthropological Series 3, Harrisburg.

Tiger, L, Shepher J.
    1974 "Women in the Kibbutz", New York: Harcourt, Brace,
    Jovanovich.

Tinker, I, and M. Bramsen.
    1975 "The Adverse Impact of Development on Women" In
    Women and World Development, edit Ed by I. Tinker and
    M.B. Bramsen, Washington, D.C. Overseas Development
    Council, Pp. 23-34.

Trigger, Bruce G.
    1959 "The Destruction of Huronia: A Study in Economic and Cul-
    tural Change, 1609-1650" Transactions of the Royal Canadian Insti-
    tute 33(1) 14-45. Ottawa.

    1962a "Trade and Tribal Warfare on the St. Lawrence in the Six-
    teenth Century", Ethnohistory 9(3): 240-256.

United Nations
    1979 "Review and Evaluation of Progress Achieved in the Imple-
    mentation of the World Plan of Action: Employment" Paper prepared
    for the World Conference of the United Nations Decade for Women.
    Copenhagen, Denmark, July 14-30, 1980. A/CONF 94/8.

Voegelin, Charles F and Erminie W. Voegelin.
    1944 "The Shawnee Female Deity in Historical Perspective" Ameri-
    can Anthropologist 46(3) 370-375.

Wallerstein, Immanuel.
1974 "The rise and future demise of the World Capitalist System: Concepts for Comparative Analysis", Comparative Studies in Society and History, 16: 387-415.

Wallace, Anthony F.C.
1969 "The Death and Rebirth of the Seneca" New York: Alfred A. Knopf.

1971 "Handsome Lake and the Decline of the Iroquois Matriarchate, In: Kinship and Culture, Francis L.K. Hsu, editor, Chicago: Adline, Pp. 367-376.

Ward, Kathryn B, editor
1984 "Women in the World-System, Its Impact on Status and Fertility", New York: Praeger Publishers.

Weist, Katherine M.
1983 "Beasts of Burden and Menial Slaves: Nineteenth Century Observations Of Northern Plains Indian Women" In: The Hidden Half, edit ed by Patrica Albers, pp. 46.

Whiting, B.B. Edwards, C.P.
1973 "A Cross-Cultural analysis of sex differences in the behavior of children aged three through 11, Journal of Social Psychology 91: 171-88.

Williams, Roger
1866 "Key into the Language of America", James H. Trunbul Editor, Publications of the Narragansett Club, 1st series, Volume 1, Providence.

Wolf, Margery
1974 "Chinese Women: Old skills in a new context"

Wright, Anne
1979a "Roles and the cultural interpretation of menopause", Papers presented at the annual meeting of the American Anthropological Association, Cincinnati, Ohio.

Zeisberger, David
1910   "History of the North American Indians", A.B. Hulbert and W.N. Schwarze, eds. Ohio Archaeological and Historical Publications, Vol. 19, pp. 1-189.

Chapter 9:

A Model for Female Status:

In this chapter I am going to propose a model for Female Status that applies to four Algonquian groups: the Wabanaki, the Delaware, the Shawnee and the Montagnais. Ethnohistoricat evidence illustrates that Females had a variety of important functions in these Native Northeastern societies and that they were important social actors who had power in the public sphere of these societies.

Here's a model for female status, which applies to all of these Northeastern groups. There are three basic parts to my model of female status. The first part of the model and a primary factor in determining female status in all of these groups is the life cycle. In each of these groups, older females who were past middle age, were the only females mentioned in the historical accounts who had individual power in the public sphere.

The second part of the model and the second primary factor that determines female status (or public power) is resource control. Each of the elder, individual females that are recorded in the historical literature had control over resources. The elder females who had public power in these groups had control over trade goods, agricultural products and goods or special knowledge of herbs and medicines. "Resources' is used in a broad sense".

The last part of the model are the structural factors that work to reinforce and maintain female status in the society. The structural factors include: matrilineal descent, matrilocal residence, male absence, rules of succession, domestic living arrangements and the presence of a female diety.

In order for females to have individual power in the public sphere of these Northeastern groups they had to have control over resources and be past middle age. Each of these primary factors of the model are interrelated and both of them worked together to provide a female with individual power in the public sphere. The structural factors of a particular society worked to maintain and reinforce collective female status. This model relates the individual female, resource control and the infrastructure of a society together to understand how, why and under what particular circumstances individual females were able to wield public power.

THE WABANAKI

The historical record on the Wabanaki discusses individual females who were known as "grand-dames" or "No-ko-musm". These females were past middle age and had a variety of privileges that younger females did not have. They also had more mobility, freedom from restraint and were able to serve in a variety of important roles in the society including functioning as political leaders, speaker's in council and serving as shamans. (Chamberlain 1902:81; 85-86) (Morrison 1983:126,127).

The historical record illustrates that a number of Wabanaki females inherited formal leadership positions. Angel Queen, a female sagamore-shaman was an elder woman who is reported to have traveled to Wabanaki villages at least twice each year. The historical record also mentioned that Angel Queen was a powerful shaman who distributed food as she traveled among the villages. Thus this individual Wabanaki female clearly was an elder woman who had control over both food resources and was reported to have strong magical power and thus had power as a shaman as well (Morrison 1983:127).

There are also several other individual females who are recorded in the historical record who clearly had individual public power. The Queen of Quacke, was a female leader who inherited her leadership position from her father (Levett 1628: 104,105). Another female who inherited a leadership position was Jacataqua of Swan Island. Jacataqua inherited the position of sagamore from her mother. Both of these females illustrate that one of the structural features present in Wabanakia that worked to reinforce and maintain female status were rules of succession that allowed individual females to inherit formal leadership positions (Griffiths 1976)(Morrison 1983)

The elder Penobscot shaman, Molly Molasses was respected and feared as a very powerful shaman. Both her age and her knowledge of herbs and medicines enabled her to obtain a position of pubic power and influence (Eckstorm 1980)

Another elder female religious leader who had great power in Micmac society was recorded by Christian missionary, Le Clercq (Le Clercq 1910). This leader was recorded as having the power to cure the sick and to protect the people from enemies. By having earned the reputation of being a powerful shaman who could cure the sick and protect people, this female was able to achieve a position of power in the public sphere of Wabanaki society.

Even though agriculture was only practiced in the Southern section of Wabanakia, females were able to obtain positions of power in the society by becoming shamans and inheriting leadership positions. The females that were recorded in the historical literature were older which enabled them to function as shamans, council speakers and political leaders only because they were able to control resources in their society. The structural organization of Wabankia aided these females by having rules of succession for political office that allowed females to inherit positions of leadership. These females were aided by this rule, but none of them would have achieved a position of power in the public sphere of the society without also being an elder who had control over resources.

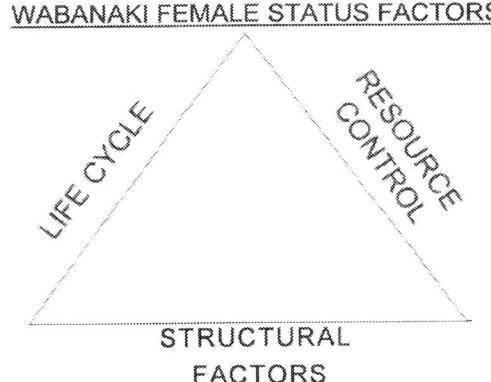

WABANAKI FEMALE STATUS FACTORS

I.   Life Cycle (age)
      a) female speakers in council meetings
      b) female shamans
      c) female political leaders
      d) female ritual warfare leaders
II. Resource Control
      a) knowledge of herbs and medicine.
III. Structural Factors
      a) rules of succession for political leadership

THE DELAWARE

Delaware females are recorded in the historical literature as serving in a number of important roles in Delaware society. Elder females and a group of young men were able to force the Esopus war captains to seek peace with the Dutch in 1664(Grumet 1980:52). Elder females were also important as shamans and traders in the society.

Here again individual females were able to attain positions of power in Delaware society only because they were older and had control over important resources like agricultural or trade goods or had shamanic curing powers. Clearly, elder female shamans who had the power to communicate with the dead, locate lost persons and foretell future events had individual power in the religious sphere of Delaware society. Also, the economic importance of Coastal Algonquian females as recorded by Mourt, Heckewelder, John Juet and a trader at Albany cannot be overlooked (Mourt 1841)(Heckewelder 1817)(Juet 1909)

Female status in Delaware society was reinforced and maintained by a number of important structural factors including: agriculture, matrilineal descent, matrilocal residence and the ritual cycle. Corn was the major staple of the Delaware diet and since females worked the garden and controlled the distribution of the agricultural products, this worked to reinforce female status in the society. Female status was also supported and reinforced by the twelve matrilineal lineages that were present in Delaware society.

These lineages regulated marriage, ceremonial obligations, feasts and the inheritance of special ritual property (Goodard 1978:225).

Individual females were very important as shamans in Delaware society and the Delaware ritual cycle also worked to maintain and reinforce female status. The two Important types of ceremonies were family feasts and vision rituals. A major ceremony was held at both corn planting and harvesting time and females played an important role in the ceremony (Goodard 1978:231,232). The matrilineal lineages conducted annual Ceremonies, which also gave, support to female status and reinforced the position of high Status for females in Delaware society.

In summary, I have argued that individual females in Delaware society achieved positions of individual power in the public sphere of the society by being older and controlling either agricultural or trade goods or by having special supernatural curing power. The high status of females in Delaware society was maintained and reinforced by the entire economic, social and ritual structure of Delaware society.

DELAWARE FEMALE STATUS FACTORS

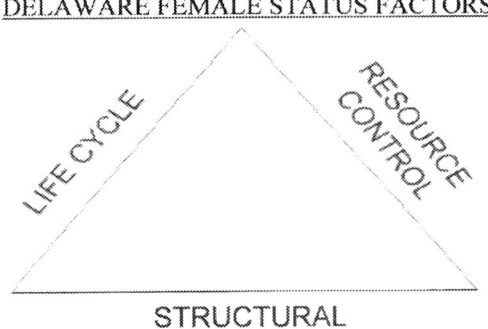

STRUCTURAL
FACTORS

I.   Life Cycle (age)
        a) female shamans
        b) female traders
II.   Resource Control
        a) agricultural goods
        b) trade goods
        c) knowledge of herbs and medicines
III.   Structural Factors
        a) matrilineal descent
        b) matrilocal residence

THE SHAWNEE

Females in Shawnee society served in a variety of functions and influenced war chiefs, supervised village affairs, directed the planting, cooking and accompaniment of the feasts. In all parts of Shawnee society where females served as important social actors in the public sphere the key elements of the model are present.

Agriculture was important in Shawnee society and it clearly worked to reinforce and maintain female status. The two distinct women's committees that directed the Bread Dance feast were the Naynahowaychki and the May-yaw-wa-thech-ki. The life Cycle (or age) was the key factor in the selection of females for the May-yaw-wa-thech-ki committee (Galloway 1934:190,191,193). The ritual Cycle itself reinforced female status in Shawnee society since the Bread Dance was a ceremony conducted for crop fertility. The females were the ones who "called" for the ceremony and the women also distributed the meat at the Feast itself.

Older women also decided the fate of Shawnee war captives and a Individual elder female could serve as a ritual war leader if she had a vision that gave her specific instructions (Trowbridge 1939:26). Here again, an individual elder female could obtain a position of power in the public sphere of Society if she also had received a vision, which gave her supernatural power.

Female status in Shawnee society was also reinforced by their religious system, which featured an important deity, called "our Grandmother" (Voeglin & Voegelin 1944).

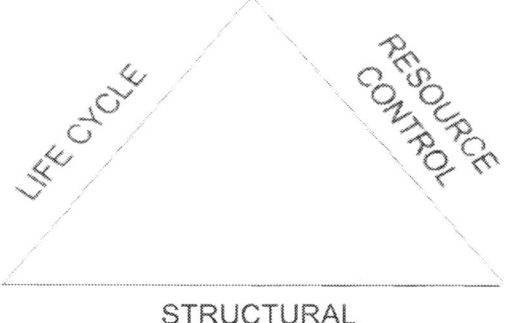

SHAWNEE FEMALE STATUS FACTORS

LIFE CYCLE

RESOURCE CONTROL

STRUCTURAL
FACTORS

I. Life Cycle (age)
    a) village supervisors
    b) power to influence male war chiefs
    c) may-yaw-wa-thech-ki bread dance committee
II. Resource Control
    a) agricultural goods and the distribution of food at feasts
    b) supernatural visions
III. Structural Factors
    a) ritual cycle (bread dance ceremony)
    b) female deity ("our Grandmother")

THE MONTAGNAIS

Montagnais females were considered to have equal status to males in the Society and personal autonomy for both sexes was reinforced by a number of structural factors present in the social structure of Montagnais society.

In Montagnais bands, each member of the group was dependent upon each other and "Obedience was owed not to any individual, but to the practical and moral order of the group" (Leacock 1981:191). Montagnais society, leadership in any particular situation was allowed to fall upon the shoulders of the individual who was most knowledgeable (Leacock 1981:191). The principal of personal autonomy for both sexes was present in Montagnais society and it was supported by a number of structural features of Montagnais social organization. There was not a rigid sexual division of labor, decisions were made by the household group, Polygny was allowed for both sexes and divorce was easy for either marriage partner. Both men and women were involved in running the household and males were also very involved with the raising of the children (Leacock 1981:192). The reciprocal exchange of goods and services in Montagnais society also worked to reinforce and maintain sexual equality in the society. Both women and men held their own feasts and the women as well as the males were involved in the torture of War captives (Leacock 1981:193). Thus the entire social structure of Montagnais society reinforced and maintained sexual equality and personal autonomy.

In Montagnais society, elder females could obtain positions of influence in the society by controlling resources. Elder females in Montagnais society functioned as both shamans and village supervisors. Elder females who had a good knowledge of herbs and medicines functioned as curers and thus obtained a position of personal influence in the society. Female village supervisors decided the course of the Montagnais bands and thus functioned as household leaders. Although there was a tendency for matrilocal residence in Montagnais society, postnuptial residence was quite flexible. The flexibility of Montagnais society is also illustrated by the fact that no formal kinship groups or clans were present (Leacock 1981:191).

Information found in the Jesuit Relations supports the structural features of Montagnais society that I have discussed. Women in the accounts are discussed as co-equals of males and are said to have great influence over their husbands. The accounts also describe the very flexible division of labor in Montagnais society, female control over their own products, and the right to divorce and polygamy for both sexes. The independence and personal autonomy of Montagnais females was deplored by Le Jeune (Thwaites Reuben 1896-1901).

Thus females in Montagnais society were equals to males and the sexual equality present in the society was reinforced and maintained by the key factors of the social structure that I have mentioned and by an economy that was based on the reciprocal exchange of goods and services between the sexes. Individual Montagnais females who were older could become powerful shamans in the society and thus wield individual influence in the society. These females were able to become shamans because of their age and special supernatural power. Elder females in Montagnais society also served as village supervisors and organized the camp and distributed the supplies.

Thus, female status in Montagnais society operated on two different levels, at the individual level, a particular female could become a shaman or village supervisor. Female status in the society as a whole was maintained by the flexible social organization and a variety of structural factors that allowed Montagnais females to be considered as co-equals with males.

All of this changed once contact with the Europeans and in particular the Missionaries began and female status at both the individual and the collective level began to decline due to European contact. Before great changes began to be imposed on Montagnais society due to missionary contact females did function in important positions as individuals and collectively females were considered to be co-equals with males. On the individual level the only females in Montagnais Society that achieved positions of power in the society were elder females who also controlled resources. On a society level, females were considered to be equal to males and the structural features of Montagnais social organization as well as the reciprocal exchange of goods and services present in the Montagnais band economy both helped to maintain and reinforce female status in Montagnais society. The model I have proposed focuses on both the individual female as well as collective female status within Montagnais society both of which must be understood in order to achieve a more accurate historical picture of how females functioned within Montagnais society.

MONTAGNAIS FEMALE STATUS FACTORS

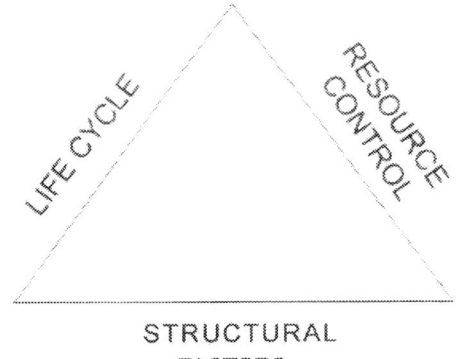

STRUCTURAL
FACTORS

I.   Life Cycle (age)
     a) female shamans
     b) female village supervisors
II.   Resource Control
     a) knowledge of herbs and medicine
     b) reciprocal exchange of goods between the sexes
III.   Structural Factors
     a) tendency for matrilocal residence
     b) both sexes had the right to divorce and practiced polygamy, both of
     these rights helped to maintain personal autonomy and sexual equality
     c) very flexible division of labor

[106]

COLLECTIVE FEMALE STATUS

THE MONTAGNAIS

Of the four Northeastern Algonquian groups discussed in this paper, females had the lowest collective status in Montagnais society, Using the term "collective female status" I am referring to situations where groups of females were important and wielded power.

As noted, Montagnais society was based on personal autonomy for both sexes and leadership was flexible and fell to a particular individual that was best suited to lead in a specific situation. Although females did obtain positions of personal power by functioning as shamans and village supervisors, Montagnais society did not have the structural features (e.g. matrilineal descent, matrilocal residence, clans) that allow for the formation of powerful groups of females.

The historical record only illustrates that individual females were important as shamans and village supervisors (Thwaites 1906:6:61, 14:183). The Infrastructure of Montagnais society was based on flexible postnuptial residence and division of labor, and personal autonomy for both sexes did not allow for the formation of group alliances. Thus the historical record stressed the importance of individual females as opposed to groups of females. This must be viewed within the context of the structural factors that was present in Montagnais society.

THE WABANAKI

Females in Wabanaki society had only slightly more collective status and power than females in Montagnais society did. The only area in Wabanaki society in which females played an important collective role was in the torture of War captives (Pierre Maillard 1758:29). Ritual torture of war captives was done by females in Wabanki society and they participated as a group in the Scalp Dance which honored specific warriors who had taken scalps or captives. Thus collective ritual reinforced female importance in the torture of war captives in Wabanki society.

Wabanki society did not have any of the structural features which contribute to the formation of powerful collective groups of females. This is not surprising since the vast majority of the historical record discusses the importance of individual Wabanaki females and not on the power or status those groups of females in Wabanaki society had.

THE SHAWNEE

Females functioned as important collective groups in several areas in Shawnee Society. Agriculture was practiced by the Shawnee and was a very important part of Shawnee subsistence. One of the areas in which Shawnee females were important as a collective group was in the Bread Dance feast which was a ceremony conducted for crop fertility. The females called the ceremony, distributed the meat at the feast and two women's committees directed the feast (Galloway 1934:190,191,193).

Shawnee females also decided the fate of Shawnee war captives. Four elder females who were the heads of the female society decided the fate of Shawnee war captives. Thus like the Wabanaki females, Shawnee females played an important part in deciding the fate of war captives (Trowbridge 1939:26).

Although collective female status was supported to a degree by the importance of agriculture in the Shawnee subsistence economy and the ritual cycle, Shawnee Society did not have the key structural factors that allow for the formation of female Alliance groups that can wield collective power.

THE DELAWARE

Females had a high degree of collective status in Delaware society because the structural factors that allow for the formation of collective groups of allied females were present. The most important features in Delaware society that supported collective female status was: matrilineal decent, matrilocal residence and the importance of agriculture.

The historical record describes a variety of areas in which females were important as collective groups. A group of females helped to force the Esopus war Captains to seek peace with the Dutch (Grumet 1980:52). This can be understood since females controlled the production and distribution of the agricultural goods that supplied the war parties.

The historical record also shows that females were important as traders in a number of coastal Algonquian groups (Grumet 1980:57). Females in Delaware Society were also able to regulate marriages, ceremonial obligations, feasts and the Inheritance of special ritual property in Delaware society because of the presence of Matrilineal lineages.

CONCLUSION

In summary, I have proposed a model of female status that focuses on both individual and collective female status. The two key components of my model of female status is the life cycle (age) and resource control. In all of these Northeastern Algonquian groups, individual females who achieved positions of power in the public sphere of society were elders who also controlled important resources (e.g. agricultural, trade or supernatural

power). All of the individual females who are cited in the Historical literature that I have discussed were elder females who controlled resources.
Thus this is a constant found among all of these groups.

The other components of my model of female status are the structural
factors those were present in these societies that functioned to maintain and
reinforce collective female status. The strength of collective female status,
or the ability of groups of females to wield public power, varied between
these Northeastern groups depending upon the particular features that were
present in each of these societies. Collective female status was low for both
the Montagnais and the Wabanaki, intermediate for the Shawnee and high
in the Delaware.

Two important areas that females participated in collectively that
have been largely ignored by secondary source accounts of these groups is
their involvement in trade and warfare. Females in Delaware society for
example functioned as important traders. Females in Wabanaki and
Shawnee society had important roles in warfare. Also, female participation
in the market-exchange economy of these Northeastern Algonquian groups
must be reevaluated because it clearly has been underestimated to date.

I also believe that research on female status is a good laboratory that
can allow the anthropologist to study the process of historical change in
Native Societies. By dong comparative research that focuses on how
female status Changed as a result of contact with the world system, a better understanding of how the social structure adapted to these changes can
be discovered.

SELECTED BIBLIOGRAPHY

Chamberlain, Montague
  1902 "The Primitive Life of the Wapanaki Women". Acadiensis 2(2)
  75-86

Eckstorm, Fannie Hardy
  1980 <u>Old John Neptune and Other Maine Indian Shamans.</u> (1945)
  Orono, Maine: The University of Maine.

Galloway, William A.
  1934 <u>Old Chillicothe: Shawnee and Pioneer History: Conflicts and
  Romances in the Northwest Territory</u> Xenia, Ohio: The Buckeye
  Press.

Goddard, Ives
  1978 "Delaware", In Handbook of North American Indians, Vol 15:
  Northeast, William C. Sturtevant and Bruce G. Trigger,
  Eds, Pp. 213-239 Washington: Smithsonian Institution.

Griffiths, Linda
  1976 Jacataqua Bates College Bulletin (Allumnus Issue) 73(6):8.

Grumet, Robert Steven
  1978a "We are not so Great Fools" Changes in Upper Delawarn
  Socio-Political Life, 1630-1758. Ph.D. dissertation, Anthropology
  Department, Rutgers University.

  1980 "Sunksquaws, Shamans, and Tradeswomen: Middle Atlantic
  Coastal Algonkian Women During the 17th and 18th Centuries"
  In: <u>Women and Colonization: Anthropological Perspectives,</u>
  Mona Etienne and Eleanor Leacock, eds. Pp. 43-62, New York:
  Praeger.

Heckewelder, John
  1817 History, Manners, and Customs of the Indian Nations,
  Philiadelphia: Historical Society of Pennsylvania.

Juet, Robert
  1909 From "The Third Voyage of Master Henry Hudson," 1610
  Pp. 11-28 in: <u>Narratives of New Netherland, 1609-1664,</u>
  J. Franklin Jameson, editor. New York: Charles Scriber's
  Sons (Reprinted: Barnes and Noble, New York 1967).

Leacock, Eleanor
1958 "Status among the Montagnais-Naskapi of Labrador"
Ethnohistory 5(3): Pp. 200-209.

1981"Seventeenth Century Montagnais Social Relations and Values"
In: Handbook of North American Indians, Vol 15 Subarctic.
William C. Sturtevant and June Helm, eds. Pp. 190-195,
Washington: Smithsonian Institution.

Le Clercq, Chrestien
1910 New Relation of Gaspesia with the Customs & Religion of the
Gaspesian Indians. Edited and trans. William F. Ganong
Toronto: The Champlain Society, Pp. 229-230.

Levett, Christopher
1628 A Voyage into New England Begun in 1623 and Ended in 1624,
Pp. 79-139 in Christopher Levett of York. The Pioneer Colonist
In Casco Bay. James P. Baxter, editor, 1893. Portland Maine:
The Gorges Society.

Maillard, Antoine Simon
1758 An account of the Customs and Manners of Micmakis and
Maricheets, London: Printed for S. Hooper and A. Morley.

Morrison, Alvin H.
1982 "Dawnland Dog-Feast: Wabanaki Warfare, and Slavery,
Ca 1600-ca 1760" A paper presented at the Canadian
Ethnology Society, Vancouver, British Columbia.

1983 "Wabanaki Women Extraordinaire: A Sampler From Fact
And Fancy" Pp. 125-136 in: Papers of the 14th Algonquian
Conference. William Cowan, editor. Ottawa: Carleton University.

Mourt, George
1841 (Orig 1622) "Mourt's Relation," In: Alexander Young, editor,
Chronicles of the Pilgrim Fathers of the Colony of Plymouth
From 1602 to 1625, Boston.

Thwaites, Reuben, G, editor
1896-1901 The Jesuit Relations and Allied Documents: Travels
And Explorations of the Jesuit Missionaries in New France, 1610-
1791, 73 Vols, Cleveland, Burrows Brothers Company.

Trowbridge, Charles C.
    1824"Traditions of the Lenee of Lenaupee or Delaware's (Manuscript) In C.C. Trowbridge Papers, Michigan Historical Collections, University of Michigan, Ann Arbor.

    1939"Shawnese Traditions", Vernon Kinietz and Erminie W. Voegelin, eds., University of Michigan Museum of Anthropology Occasional Contributions 9. Ann Arbor.

Voegelin, Charles F, and Erminie W. Voegelin
    1935 "Shawnee Name Groups", American Anthropologist 37 (4): 617-635.
    1944 "The Shawnee Female Deity in Historical Perspective", American Anthropologist 46(3): 370-375.

About the Authors

David A. Ezzo has been involved with the study of Native American Indian history and culture for over twenty-five years. His interest in the subject matter first began when he earned his Indian Lore badge from Mr. Ronald P. Koch when he was 15 years old.

His interest in the topic continued when he served as an Indian Lore counselor at Camp Turner for four summers in 1979, 1980, 1981, and 1983.

David began his academic study of Native Americans when he earned a BA degree in Anthropology from SUNY Fredonia in 1985. While at Fredonia he wrote two published articles and co-wrote a third article with one of his professors, Dr. Alvin H. Morrison. This article was presented at the 16th Algonquian Conference and was published one year later in 1986.

David earned his MA in Anthropology from the University of Oklahoma in 1987. During his time at the University of Oklahoma he presented several papers including one at a Frontier Conference at OU in 1986 and also a paper at an Algonquian Conference. His MA thesis was also written on a Native American Indian topic. The title of his thesis "Female Status in Northeastern North America" was an historical survey of the roles of Native America women in a number of Algonquian societies.

During subsequent years David continued to attend and publish papers at Algonquian Conferences. He also continued to serve as a BSA Indian Lore merit badge counselor.

In 2005 David earned his Ph.D in Anthropology from Richardson University. Also in August of 2005 he was appointed as an Adjunct Professor of Anthropology at Erie Community College (North Campus) where he taught an Introduction to Sociology course.

David Ezzo and Michael Moskowitz have co-written several articles together including one article on Delaware Indian history and Land Claims cases, and one on the Stockbridge-Munsee land claims case and also a paper on Black Beaver, a Delaware Indian Chief.

Michael Moskowitz has had a life long interest in history, politics, law and genealogy. In 1988 he received a Bachelor of Arts Degree in Political Science with a minor in History from The George Washington University in Washington, D.C. and in 1991, a Juris Doctorate from American University-Washington College of Law, also in Washington, D.C. It was during law school that Michael studied the legal issues concerning American Indians and began researching this area in depth. While in Washington, Michael served as a volunteer Law Clerk for the Native American Rights Fund where he worked on several issues concerning several American Indian tribes located in the North East United States. Michael, along with co-author David Ezzo, has had several articles on legal-historical topics as they relate to specific native groups of the North East United States, published that were presented at the Algonquian Studies Group. Michael founded and ran his own consulting firm dedicated to American Indian affairs for several years. He has been a volunteer with the Boy Scouts of America for many years, in which among other things he teaches Scouts about American Indian history. He currently lives with his wife Beth in suburban Long Island, New York.

Printed in the United States
110187LV00001B/61-69/A